D0187968

PENGUIN
COMPASS

THE PATH TO TRANQUILITY

Tenzin Gyatso, His Holiness the Fourteenth Dalai Lama and winner of the 1989 Nobel Peace Prize, is recognized internationally as a spiritual leader and peace statesman. The recipient of numerous honorary degrees and humanitarian awards, he lives in Dharamsala, India.

Renuka Singh has a doctorate in sociology from Jawaharlal Nehru University, New Delhi. She is a Fellow at the Center for Study of Social Systems.

The Path to Tranquility

DAILY WISDOM

HIS HOLINESS THE DALAI LAMA

COMPILED AND EDITED BY

RENUKA SINGH

WITH A FOREWORD BY

THE DALAI LAMA

PENGUIN COMPASS

PENGUIN COMPASS
Published by the Penguin Group
Penguin Putnam Inc., 375 Hudson Street, New York, New York 10014, U.S.A.
Penguin Books Ltd, 80 Strand, London WC2R 0RL, England
Penguin Books Australia Ltd, 250 Camberwell Road,
Camberwell, Victoria 3124, Australia
Penguin Books Canada Ltd, 10 Alcorn Avenue, Toronto, Ontario, Canada M4V 3B2
Penguin Books India (P) Ltd, 11 Community Centre,
Panchsheel Park, New Delhi – 110 017, India
Penguin Books (N.Z.) Ltd, Cnr Rosedale and Airborne Roads,
Albany, Auckland, New Zealand
Penguin Books (South Africa) (Pty) Ltd, 24 Sturdee Avenue,
Rosebank, Johannesburg 2196, South Africa

Penguin Books Ltd, Registered Offices: Harmondsworth, Middlesex, England

First published in India by Penguin Books India 1998
First published in the United States of America by Viking Arkana,
a member of Penguin Putnam Inc. 1999
Published in Penguin Compass 2002

1   3   5   7   9   10   8   6   4   2

Copyright © His Holiness The Dalai Lama, 1998
All rights reserved

Pages v.–vi. constitute an extension of this copyright page.

THE LIBRARY OF CONGRESS HAS CATALOGED THE AMERICAN HARDCOVER EDITION AS FOLLOWS:
Bstan-'dzin-rgya-mtsho, Dalai Lama XIV, 1935–
The path to tranquility : daily wisdom by the Dalai Lama / compiled
and edited by Renuka Singh ; with a foreword by the Dalai Lama.
p.   cm.
ISBN 0-670-88759-5 (hc.)
ISBN 0 14 01.9612 9 (pbk.)
1. Buddhist devotional calendars.   2. Buddhist meditations.
I. Singh, Renuka, 1953–   II. Title.
BQ5580.B77   1999
294.3'4432—dc21   99-35039

Printed in the United States of America
Set in Goudy Newstyle
Designed by Francesca Belanger

Except in the United States of America, this book is sold subject to the
condition that it shall not, by way of trade or otherwise, be lent, re-sold, hired out,
or otherwise circulated without the publisher's prior consent in any form of binding
or cover other than that in which it is published and without a similar condition
including this condition being imposed on the subsequent purchaser.

Acknowledgments

Grateful acknowledgment is made for permission to reprint the following copyright material:

From *Gentle Bridges* by Jeremy W. Hayward and Francisco J. Varela. Copyright © 1992 by Francisco J. Varela and Jeremy W. Hayward. Reprinted by arrangement with Shambhala Publications Inc., Boston.

From *A Flash of Lightning in the Dark of Night* by the Dalai Lama. © 1994 by Association Bouddhiste des Centres de Dordogne. Reprinted by arrangement with Shambhala Publications Inc., Boston.

From *Violence and Compassion: Conversations with the Dalai Lama*, translated by Jean Claude Carriere. Translation copyright © 1996, Doubleday a division of Bantam Doubleday Dell Publishing Group. Used by permission of Doubleday, a division of Bantam Doubleday Dell Publishing Group, Inc.

From *Mandala* magazine. Reprinted by arrangement with Foundation for the Preservation of the Mahayana Tradition (FPMT) International Office, California, publisher of *Mandala* magazine.

From *Kindness, Clarity and Insight*, edited by Jeffrey Hopkins and Elizabeth Napper, Copyright © 1984 by Tenzin Gyatso and Jeffrey Hopkins; *Path of the Bodhisattva Warrior*, compiled and translated by Glenn H. Mullin, Copyright © 1988 by Glenn H. Mullin; *Path to Bliss*, edited by Christine Cox, 1991; *The Dalai*

Lama: A Policy of Kindness, compiled and edited by Sidney Piburn, (second edition), 1993; and *Healing Anger* by The Dalai Lama, 1997. Reprinted by arrangement with Snow Lion Publications, New York.

From *Generous Wisdom*, edited by Dexter Roberts, 1992; *Dialogues on Universal Responsibility and Education* by H.H. the Dalai Lama, 1995; *Opening the Mind and Generating a Good Heart* by H.H. the Dalai Lama, 1995 (4th edition). Reprinted by arrangement with the Library of Tibetan Works and Archives, Dharamsala.

From *Collected Statements, Interviews and Articles: H.H. the XIV Dalai Lama*, 1986. Reprinted by arrangement with the Department of Information and International Relations, Dharamsala.

From *Mind Science* by the Dalai Lama, 1991; *The Dalai Lama: The Meaning of Life*, edited by Jeffrey Hopkins, 1992; *The World of Tibetan Buddhism* by the Dalai Lama, edited by Geshe Thupten Jinpa, 1995; *The Good Heart* by H.H. the Dalai Lama, edited by Robert Kiely, 1996; *Sleeping, Dreaming and Dying*, edited by Francisco J. Varela, 1997. Reprinted by arrangement with Wisdom Publications, New York.

From *Freedom in Exile: The Autobiography of His Holiness, The Dalai Lama of Tibet*. Copyright © 1990 by Tenzin Gyatso. Reprinted by permission of HarperCollins Publishers, Inc.

From *Worlds in Harmony* by the Dalai Lama with Daniel Goleman et al, © 1992. Published by Parallax Press, California.

From *Dharma Celebration Lectures*. Reprinted by arrangement with Tushita Mahayana Meditation Centre, Delhi.

Contents

Foreword

As human beings, we all want to be happy and to avoid suffering. In my limited experience, if we are to achieve this, it is immensely valuable to be able to cultivate and maintain a positive state of mind. In the Buddhist tradition to which I belong, one of the most effective means of doing so is to engage in meditation. Although meditation can sometimes mean sitting in a particular formal posture and stilling the mind, it can also include continuously familiarizing ourselves with positive thoughts. This is why we regularly read and recite the texts of scriptures and prayers. I have drawn great inspiration over the years from a short work called *Eight Verses for Training the Mind*. It contains much useful advice, counseling us always to consider others as more important than ourselves, to face and oppose the disturbing emotions that endanger our peace of mind, and to give whatever benefit arises to others while shouldering whatever difficulties occur on ourselves.

This book contains daily quotations selected from my own writings and published works. I humbly pray that readers may find some inspiration in these words to develop that warmhearted peace of mind that is the key to enduring happiness.

His Holiness the Dalai Lama
February 26, 1998

Editor's Note

This book is a compilation of daily thoughts by His Holiness the Dalai Lama. It also forms a part of His Holiness's contribution to the preservation of the ancient Indian wisdom-culture. My publisher originally proposed the idea behind this book and His Holiness gave his approval and blessing. I began working on it without delay at the beginning of last year.

I am acutely aware of the principle of selectivity unfolding here. The quotations are my selections from His Holiness's writings, teachings, and occasional interviews. These, I hope, will properly reflect His Holiness's spiritual and secular concerns and spread his message of universal responsibility, compassion, and peace. Also, through these quotations, I intend to share with nonspecialized audiences and Dharma students the different vistas and possibilities that opened before me, and the apparently simple yet complex core of His Holiness's essential thoughts. However, one must bear in mind that terms such as "listening," "giving," "thinking," "meditating," etc., are processual and should be perceived in the context of the Buddhist practice of cultivating *bodhicitta*—the aspiration to attain enlightenment for the benefit of all.

In the foreword, His Holiness very aptly refers to the

Eight Verses for Training the Mind. Based on my personal experiences, I can also vouch for their unfailing usefulness and would like to present the verses here:

Regarding all sentient beings
As excelling even the wish-granting gem
For accomplishing the highest aim,
May I always hold them most dear.

When in the company of others
I shall always consider myself the lowest of all,
And from the depth of my heart
Hold them dear and supreme.

Vigilant, the moment a delusion appears,
Which endangers myself and others,
I shall confront and avert it
Without delay.

When I see beings of wicked nature
overwhelmed by violent negative actions and
    sufferings,
I shall hold such rare ones dear,
As if I have found a precious treasure.

When others, out of envy, treat me with abuse,
Insult me or the like,
I shall accept defeat,
And offer the victory to others.

When someone I have benefited
And in whom I have great hopes
Gives me terrible harm,
I shall regard him as my holy spiritual friend.

In short, both directly and indirectly, do I offer
Every benefit and happiness to all sentient beings,
    my mothers;
May I secretly take upon myself
All their harmful actions and suffering.

May they not be defiled by the concepts
Of the eight profane concerns.
And aware that all things are illusory,
May they, ungrasping, be freed from bondage.

I am deeply indebted to my teacher and friend His Holiness Tenzin Gyatso, the fourteenth Dalai Lama, for his support and blessings for this project. For all his cooperation and patience, Tenzin Geyche Tethong deserves a special thanks. I also owe thanks to Lhakdor for his promptness in providing me with His Holiness's unpublished material and for his valuable suggestions.

I extend my gratitude to Linda and Ashok Jhalani, Antonella and Naresh Mathur, and Alison Ramsey for confirming some of my selections in this book. Also to Prama and Ranji Bhandari for their moral support, and to Sunita Kakaria for taking care of me in McLeod Ganj. I would also like to acknowledge the help rendered by V. K. Karthika and Sudeshna Shome Ghosh from Penguin. They have been working painstakingly on this project with me. At the eleventh hour, receiving financial support from Derek Goh for seeking permission to publish the selected quotations came as a real surprise. I am grateful to him for not letting this project fall apart.

Finally, thanks to my family members Pritam Singh, Jyoti and Paul, Ashma and Tsagaadai, and Sumeet and Supriti for their support that allowed me to devote so much time to my work.

This work is dedicated to all sentient beings with a wish for their welfare and happiness.

Renuka Singh
April 1998

The Path to Tranquility

January

JANUARY 1

I love friends, I want more friends. I love smiles. That is a fact. How to develop smiles? There are a variety of smiles. Some smiles are sarcastic. Some smiles are artificial—diplomatic smiles. These smiles do not produce satisfaction, but rather fear or suspicion. But a genuine smile gives us hope, freshness.

If we want a genuine smile, then first we must produce the basis for a smile to come.

If you have fear of some pain or suffering, you should examine whether there is anything you can do about it. If you can, there is no need to worry about it; if you cannot do anything, then also there is no need to worry.

JANUARY 3

To be aware of a single shortcoming within oneself is more useful than to be aware of a thousand in somebody else. Rather than speaking badly about people and in ways that will produce friction and unrest in their lives, we should practice a purer perception of them, and when we speak of others, speak of their good qualities.

If you find yourself slandering anybody, first imagine that your mouth is filled with excrement. It will break you of the habit quickly enough.

If you are mindful of death, it will not come as a surprise—you will not be anxious. You will feel that death is merely like changing your clothes. Consequently, at that point you will be able to maintain your calmness of mind.

To foster inner awareness, introspection, and reasoning is more efficient than meditation and prayer.

Right from the moment of our birth, we are under the care and kindness of our parents and then later on in our life when we are oppressed by sickness and become old, we are again dependent on the kindness of others.

Since at the beginning and end of our lives we are so dependent on others' kindness, how can it be that in the middle we neglect kindness toward others?

*S*cientific research and development should work together with meditative research and development since both are concerned with similar objects. The one proceeds through experiment by instruments and the other through inner experience and meditation.

A clear distinction should be made between what is not found by science and what is found to be nonexistent by science. What science finds to be nonexistent, we must accept as nonexistent; but what science merely does not find is a completely different matter. . . . It is quite clear that there are many, many mysterious things.

All of the different religious faiths, despite their philosophical differences, have a similar objective. Every religion emphasizes human improvement, love, respect for others, sharing other people's suffering. On these lines every religion has more or less the same viewpoint and the same goal.

*P*hysically you are a human being, but mentally you are incomplete. Given that we have this physical human form, we must safeguard our mental capacity for judgment. For that, we cannot take out insurance; the insurance company is within: self-discipline, self-awareness, and a clear realization of the disadvantages of anger and the positive effects of kindness.

In the case of one individual or person like myself, the practice of compassion and religion coincides. But another individual, without religion, can practice spirituality without being religious. So, a secular person can be spiritual.

Compassion is compulsory for everyone to practice, and if I were a dictator I would dictate to everyone to do so.

JANUARY 11

I think religion, ideology, economy, and political systems are all man's creation. Since they are man's creation, they must relate with human feeling and the human spirit. If they are practiced with human feeling, they fulfill some basic human aspirations. The various religions and ideologies are meant for humanity and not the opposite.

Material progress alone is not sufficient to achieve an ideal society. Even in countries where great external progress has been made, mental problems have increased. No amount of legislation or coercion can accomplish the well-being of society, for this depends upon the internal attitude of the people who comprise it. Therefore, mental development, in harmony with material development, is very important.

The human level of mental development is not complete. Even in the ordinary sense, within our inner state there are still many things to explore. This has nothing to do with religious ideology; this is spiritual. Some part of the brain's capability may be fully utilized only through deep meditation. But in the meantime, things can be explored in the ordinary way. So from that viewpoint, the human being is unfinished.

*S*ometimes one creates a dynamic impression by saying something, and sometimes one creates as significant an impression by remaining silent.

All living beings, starting from insects, want happiness and not suffering. However, we are only one, whereas others are infinite in number. Thus, it can be clearly decided that others gaining happiness is more important than just yourself alone.

JANUARY 16

If during the dreaming state you direct your awareness and your concentration to the throat, this will make your dreams clearer. Whereas, if you direct your awareness to the heart, then it will make your sleep deeper. So here is a subjective sleeping pill.

JANUARY 17

It would be much more constructive if people tried to understand their supposed enemies. Learning to forgive is much more useful than merely picking up a stone and throwing it at the object of one's anger, the more so when the provocation is extreme. For it is under the greatest adversity that there exists the greatest potential for doing good, both for oneself and others.

*T*o develop patience, you need someone who willfully hurts you. Such people give us real opportunities to practice tolerance. They test our inner strength in a way that even our guru cannot. Basically, patience protects us from being discouraged.

JANUARY 19

Whether in remote places or densely populated cities, we work and struggle for the same fundamental purpose. While doing so, we fail to realize that it is important to follow the correct method in achieving our goal—for the method is all important.

When a faulty deed has been done, after learning that it was wrong one can engage in disclosure of the faulty deed (in the presence of actual or imagined holy beings) and develop an intention not to do that action again in the future. This diminishes the force of the ill deed.

On the basis of external action, it is difficult to distinguish whether an action is violent or nonviolent. Basically it depends on the motivation behind the action.

If the motivation is negative, even though the external appearance may be very smooth and gentle, in a deeper sense the action is very violent. On the contrary, harsh actions and words done with a sincere, positive motivation are essentially nonviolent.

In other words, violence is a destructive power. Nonviolence is constructive.

I tell my generation that we were born during the darkest period in our long history. There is a big challenge and it is very unfortunate. But if there is a challenge then there is an opportunity to face it, an opportunity to demonstrate our will and our determination. So from that viewpoint I think that our generation is fortunate.

JANUARY 23

To develop genuine devotion, you must know the meaning of teachings. The main emphasis in Buddhism is to transform the mind, and transformation depends on meditation. In order to meditate correctly you must have knowledge, and communities, too, must be uplifted through knowledge.

Kindness is the key to peace and harmony in family life. Families in exile must educate their children. They should be their first lama.

A blossoming tree becomes bare and stripped in autumn. Beauty changes into ugliness, youth into old age, and fault into virtue. Things do not remain the same and nothing really exists. Thus, appearances and emptiness exist simultaneously.

Determination, courage, and self-confidence are the key factors for success. In spite of obstacles and difficulties, if we have firm determination, we can work them out. Whatever the circumstances, we should remain humble, modest, and without pride.

We can hardly call a beggar an obstacle to generosity.

*S*imply being praised is of no substantial help at all: it does not increase people's good fortune, nor does it make them live any longer. If temporary pleasure is all you want, you might as well take drugs. Yet many people invest much money and even deceive their friends to win status. This is quite stupid. Their status and fame do not really help much in this life and do nothing for future lives. There is no point in being happy if we are famous, or unhappy because people speak ill of us.

JANUARY 29

It is said that if you want to know what you were doing in the past, look at your body now; if you want to know what will happen to you in the future, look at what your mind is doing now.

Religion involves practice of methods and modes conducive to the realization of serenity, discipline, joyous detachment, and self-control. It should be observed that normally it is through the inattentive body, speech, and mind that all harmful and unethical conditions are created. Therefore, it naturally presupposes that the pacification, training, and taming of the physical, mental, and verbal activities are of fundamental importance.

To sum up, it is essential first of all to rectify, nullify, and put a stop to all physical misconduct, followed by that of speech.

*P*oliticians need religion even more than a hermit in retreat. If a hermit acts out of bad motivation, he harms no one but himself. But if someone who can directly influence the whole of society acts with bad motivation, then a great number of people will be adversely affected.

February

To renounce the world means to give up your attachment to the world. It does not mean that you have to separate yourself from it. The very purpose of our doctrine is to serve others. In order to serve others you must remain in the society. You should not isolate yourself from the rest.

Human happiness and human satisfaction must ultimately come from within oneself. It is wrong to expect some final satisfaction to come from money or from a computer.

According to Buddhist practice, basically there are three stages or steps. The initial stage is to reduce attachment toward life. The second stage is the elimination of desire and attachment to this samsara. Then in the third stage, self-cherishing is eliminated. As a result of rigorous practice I feel there is a possibility of cessation; i.e., nirvana.

*T*rue compassion is not just an emotional response but a firm commitment founded on reason. Therefore, a truly compassionate attitude toward others does not change even if they behave negatively. Through universal altruism, you develop a feeling of responsibility for others: the wish to help them actively overcome their problems.

*F*or discovering one's true inner nature, I think one should try to take out some time, with quiet and relaxation, to think more inwardly and to investigate the inner world. That may help. Then when one is very much involved in hatred or attachment, if there is time or possibility during that very moment, just try to look inward and ask: "What is attachment? What is the nature of anger?"

*S*uffering increases your inner strength. Also, the wishing for suffering makes the suffering disappear.

If the basic human nature was aggressive, we would have been born with animal claws and huge teeth—but ours are very short, very pretty, very weak! That means we are not well equipped to be aggressive beings. Even the size of our mouth is very small. So I think the basic nature of human beings should be gentle.

During conception, even the physical substance on which the self is conventionally based—the egg and sperm—belongs to someone else, the parents; still you can say that it belongs to the self also. The body comes from someone else, but as soon as the consciousness enters, it's that new person's body, embryo, fetus, or whatever you want to call it, even though prior to that it wasn't. So the physical constituents of the embryo come from two different people; but as soon as the consciousness enters the mixed cell, that cell now belongs to the consciousness.

As long as you are not completely enlightened there will always be an inner obstruction to knowledge that will make your task of helping others incomplete.

Among the 5.7 billion human beings, the older generation, including me, is getting ready to say goodbye to this world. The youth has to carry the responsibility for the future. So, please realize your responsibility, remember your potential, and have self-confidence. Have an open mind and a sense of caring and belonging. The freshness and strength that youth has should not fade away. You must keep this enthusiasm.

Laziness will stop your progress in your spiritual practice. One can be deceived by three types of laziness: the laziness of indolence, which is the wish to procrastinate; the laziness of inferiority, which is doubting your capabilities; and the laziness that is attachment to negative actions, or putting great effort into nonvirtue.

*I*deally, one should have a great deal of courage and strength, but not boast or make a big show of it. Then, in times of need, one should rise to the occasion and fight bravely for what is right.

FEBRUARY 13

*S*ome people, sweet and attractive, and strong and healthy, happen to die young. They are masters in disguise teaching us about impermanence.

We practice various meditations during dream states. The potential of such practices is that at a certain level it is possible to separate the gross levels of consciousness from the gross physical state, and arrive at a subtler level of mind and body. You could, for example, separate your mind from your body during sleep and do some extra work that you cannot do in your ordinary body. However, you might not get paid for it!

Our state of mind plays a major role in our day-to-day experiences as well as our physical and mental well-being. If a person has a calm and stable mind, this influences his or her attitude and behavior in relation to others. In other words, if someone remains in a peaceful and tranquil state of mind, external surroundings can cause them only a limited disturbance.

Nearly all of us receive our first lessons in peaceful living from our mothers, because the need for love lies at the very foundation of human existence. From the earliest stages of our growth, we are completely dependent on our mother's care and it is very important for us that she express her love. If children do not receive proper affection, in later life they will often find it hard to love others.

If objects and people evoke attachment in us, we do not understand the true nature of phenomena. We can only become detached by realizing the true nature of things.

Here is a general statement about Tibetan medicine: Human physiology is spoken of in terms of the three humors—wind, bile, and phlegm. Where do disturbances originate? Wind, bile, and phlegm imbalances occur respectively from the "three poisons," or primary mental afflictions; namely, attachment, anger, and ignorance.

Both bondage and true freedom depend on the varying states of the clear light mind. The state that meditators try to attain through the application of various meditative techniques is one in which this ultimate nature of mind fully manifests all its positive potential.

Every noble work is bound to face problems and obstacles. It is important to check your goal and motivation thoroughly. One should be very truthful, honest, and reasonable. One's action should be good for others, and for oneself as well.

Once a positive goal is chosen, you should decide to pursue it all the way to the end. Even if it is not realized, at least there will be no regret.

*E*verything has its limits. Too much consumption or effort to make money is not good. Neither is too much contentment. In principle, contentment should be pursued, but pure contentment is almost suicidal.

What irritates us in the first place is that our wishes are not fulfilled. But remaining upset does nothing to help fulfill those wishes. So we neither fulfill our wishes nor regain our cheerfulness!

This disconcerted state, from which anger can grow, is most dangerous. We should try never to let our happy frame of mind be disturbed. Whether we are suffering at present or have suffered in the past, there is no reason to be unhappy.

When you have fear, you can think: "Others have fear similar to this; may I take to myself all of their fears." Even though you are opening yourself to greater suffering, taking greater hardship on yourself, your fear lessens.

In this ever-changing world there are two important things that we should keep in mind.

The first is self-examination. We should reexamine our own attitude toward others and constantly check ourselves to see whether we are practicing properly. Before pointing our finger at others we should point it toward ourselves.

Second, we must be prepared to admit our faults and stand corrected.

Your experience will enable you to understand what "consciousness" implies and what it is. Consciousness is a nonobstructing phenomenon, is nonmaterial, and has the quality of luminosity; that is, it reflects any object by arising in the aspect of that object.

Consciousness is like a crystal stone; while a crystal is resting on a colored surface you cannot see the real untinted clarity of the crystal stone, but once you take the crystal away from the surface you can perceive its actual clarity.

Individuals who are best suited for practice are those who are not only intellectually gifted, but also have single-pointed faith and dedication, and are wise. These people are most receptive to spiritual practice.

In the second group, individuals may not be highly intelligent but they have a rock-solid foundation in faith. The unfortunate are those in the third category.

Although these individuals may be highly intelligent, they are always dogged by scepticism and doubts. They are clever, but they tend to be hesitant and sceptical and are never really able to settle down. These people are the least receptive.

If you want to change the world, first try to improve and bring about change within yourself. That will help change your family. From there it just gets bigger and bigger. Everything we do has some effect, some impact.

*T*he idea that our interactions with others actually help our own insight is quite interesting. In an intimate relationship, where love and attachment are mixed, it is difficult to say how this will help the individual who is practicing.

In a case where there is attachment or clinging to another person, where the person is arising as a very strong object and the attachment is arising with a strong sense of "I"—"I love this person, I am grasping for this person"—if you see this as a false idea of self, you can have some insight into the notion of emptiness.

A nagging sense of discontent, a feeling of being dissatisfied, or of something being not right, is the fuel that gives rise to anger and hatred. This discontent arises in us when we feel that either we ourselves, or someone we love, or our close friends are being treated unfairly or threatened and that people are being unjust.

Also, when others somehow obstruct us in achieving something, we feel that we are being trodden upon, and then we feel angry. So the approach here is to get at the root, appreciating the causal nexus, the chain, which will ultimately explode in an emotional state like anger or hatred.

March

Whether one believes in a religion or not, and whether one believes in rebirth or not, there isn't anyone who doesn't appreciate kindness and compassion.

When we consider that everything we experience results from a complex interplay of causes and conditions, we find that there is no single thing to desire or resent and it is more difficult for the afflictions of attachment and anger to arise. In this way the view of interdependence makes our minds more relaxed and open.

On the subject of love and marriage, my simple opinion is that making love is all right, but for marriage, don't hurry, be cautious. Make sure you will remain together forever, at least for this whole life. That is important, for if you marry hurriedly without understanding well what you are doing, then after a month or after a year, trouble starts and you will be seeking divorce. From a legal viewpoint divorce is possible, and without children maybe it is acceptable, but with children, it is not.

When we contemplate death and the impermanence of life, our minds automatically begin to take an interest in spiritual achievements, just as an ordinary person becomes apprehensive when seeing the corpse of a friend. Meditation on death cuts off attraction toward transient and meaningless activities.

Try to develop a deep conviction that the present human body has great potential and that you shall never waste even a single minute of its use.

Not taking any essence of this precious human existence, but just wasting it, is almost like taking poison while being fully aware of the consequences of doing so.

It is very wrong for people to feel deeply sad when they lose some money, yet when they waste the precious moments of their lives they do not have the slightest feeling of repentance.

The world today is engulfed in conflicts and sufferings to such an extent that everyone longs for peace and happiness; that longing has unfortunately led them to be carried away by the pursuit of ephemeral pleasures. But there are a few learned people who, dissatisfied by what is ordinarily seen or experienced, think more deeply and search for true happiness. I believe that the search for Truth will continue and will grow even keener as we make greater material progress.

*H*uman potential is the same for all. Your feeling, "I am of no value," is wrong. Absolutely wrong. You are deceiving yourself. We all have the power of thought—so what are you lacking? If you have willpower, then you can do anything. It is usually said that you are your own master.

We need to develop patience but impatience can also be conducive for such activities as cleaning and walking. With this mind of impatience one can become a woman or man of action. However, for bigger problems, patience is crucial.

If one's life is simple, contentment has to come. Simplicity is extremely important for happiness. Having few desires, feeling satisfied with what you have, is very vital: satisfaction with just enough food, clothing, and shelter to protect yourself from the elements. And finally, there is an intense delight in abandoning faulty states of mind and in cultivating helpful ones in meditation.

MARCH 10

According to the Latin root of the word, "religion" would mean "to bind again." Now how does the concept of binding or tying up come to be applied as the common term for all our various teachings?

The common enemy of all religious disciplines, the target of all moral precepts laid down by the great teachers of mankind, is selfishness of mind. For it is just this which causes ignorance, anger, and passion—which are at the root of all the troubles of the world.

According to tantra, the ultimate nature of mind is essentially pure. This pristine nature is technically called "clear light." When this clear light nature of mind is veiled or inhibited from expressing its true essence by the conditioning of afflictive emotions and thoughts, the person is said to be caught in the cycle of existence, samsara. But when, by applying appropriate meditative techniques and practices, the individual is able to fully experience this clear light nature of mind, free from the influence of the afflictive states, he or she is on the way to true liberation and full enlightenment.

Subconscious anger, if it has a parallel in Buddhist writings, would have more to do with what is called mental unhappiness or dissatisfaction, in the sense that they are regarded as the sources of anger and hostility. We can see it in terms of a lack of awareness, as well as an active misconstruing of reality.

MARCH 13

Compassion, tolerance, and altruism bring us happiness and calmness. Therefore, these are basically spiritual. Religion comes later. Actually, religion is meant for satisfaction and is the ultimate source of happiness. It simply tries to strengthen the element of mental happiness. Perhaps positive mental thought is my conception of spirituality.

MARCH 14

*T*oday our knowledge has expanded greatly with the help of science and technology. But knowledge regarding our own mind, our deep nature, is still limited in the Western world. This is because consciousness is formless and cannot be touched and so cannot be measured with instruments. It can only be known through meditation and other methods.

MARCH 15

We find that between the past and the future there is an extremely thin line—something that cannot really withstand analysis. Past and future exist in relation to the present. But if the present cannot be posited, how can past and future be posited? This is a demonstration of dependent origination.

MARCH 16

At the moment when strong feelings of anger arise, no matter how hard one tries to adopt a dignified pose, one's face looks rather ugly. The vibration that person sends is very hostile. People can sense it, and it is almost as if one can feel steam coming out of that person's body.

Indeed, not only are human beings capable of sensing it, but pets and other animals also try to avoid that person at that instant.

MARCH 17

If the evolution of the human species is entirely a matter of the environment and the modification of genes, chromosomes, and so forth, then there really isn't place for karma at all. It simply wouldn't fit because all the effects would presumably be entirely accounted for by their physical constituents.

However, cells evolve to become more and more complex and then later evolve into human beings. There are many options, some seventy trillion, that one human could become, based on the assortment of the parental genes. Yet just one option is taken, and if the question is asked—why?—then karma is directly related to this question.

MARCH 18

Happiness is a state of mind. With physical comforts if your mind is still in a state of confusion and agitation, it is not happiness. Happiness means calmness of mind.

*S*exual desire, by definition, wants something: the satisfaction of desire by the possession of the other. To a large extent this is a mental projection, provoked by a certain emotion: we imagine the other in our possession.

At the moment of desire everything seems agreeable and desirable. One sees no obstacle to it, no reason for restraint. The object desired seems to have no defects, to be worthy of all praise. But then everything changes with possession.

Once the desire disappears—whether it considers itself satisfied, or time passes and weakens it—we no longer look at the other in the same way. Some people admit they are stunned by this. Each one discovers the true nature of the other. That is why there are so many broken marriages, quarrels, lawsuits, and so much hatred.

The image we have of ourselves readily tends to be complacent. We look at ourselves with indulgence. When something unpleasant happens to us, we always have the tendency to cast the blame on others, or on fate, a demon, or a god. We shrink from descending into ourselves, as the Buddha recommended.

It looks like there is an awful lot of work to do. If you had to analyze all your dreams there would be no time left to dream.

If an individual has a sufficient spiritual base, he won't let himself be overwhelmed by the lure of technology and by the madness of possession. He or she will know how to find the right balance, without asking for too much, and know how to say: I have a camera, that's enough, I don't want another. The constant danger is to open the door to greed, one of our most relentless enemies. It is here that the real work of the mind is put into practice.

*F*or a bodhisattva to be successful in accomplishing the practice of the six perfections—generosity, ethical discipline, tolerance, joyous effort, concentration, and wisdom—cooperation with and kindness toward fellow beings are extremely important.

Years back when I drove along the road to the airport or somewhere else, I never saw chickens in the streets or in the shop fronts of stores or restaurants. Now I see them everywhere.

But why these rows of slaughtered chickens? Although it is impossible to be a total vegetarian in Tibet, I find killing animals repugnant. As far as possible I eat only vegetables and fruits.

The mind, whose nature we realize in order to actualize omniscience, must be a very special type of mind, which, in terms of its continuity, is eternal. It cannot be any other type of mind.

Because the various contaminated states of mind, such as delusions and afflictive emotional and cognitive states are adventitious, they are occasional: they arise in a certain moment but soon disappear and are not enduring.

Suffering originates from various causes and conditions. But the root cause of our pain and suffering lies in our own ignorant and undisciplined state of mind. The happiness we seek can be attained only through the purification of our minds.

In our world, we need a clear awareness of the interdependent nature of nations, of humans and animals, and of humans, animals, and the world. Everything is of interdependent nature. I feel that many problems, especially man-made problems, are due to a lack of knowledge about this interdependent nature.

MARCH 28

It is because of the intimate relationship between mind and body, and the existence of special physiological centers within our body, that physical yoga exercises and the application of special meditative techniques aimed at training the mind can have positive effects on health.

To stop being born in cyclic existence, meditate on the path; even if your head is on fire engage in practice and don't take time to put out the fire.

When we take the Buddha as an authority, as a reliable teacher, we do so on the basis of having investigated and examined his principal teaching, the Four Noble Truths. It is after having investigated the validity and reliability of this doctrine that we accept the Buddha, who propounded it, as a reliable teacher.

One important type of charity is the giving of material things such as food, clothing, and shelter to others, but it is limited, for it does not bring complete satisfaction. Just as our own experience confirms that through gradual purification of our minds more and more happiness develops, so it is the same for others; thus it is crucial that they understand what they should adopt in practice in order to achieve happiness. To facilitate their learning these topics, we need to be fully capable of teaching them.

April

APRIL 1

It is necessary to help others, not only in our prayers, but in our daily lives. If we find we cannot help others, the least we can do is to desist from harming them.

APRIL 2

The observation that good people suffer, and evil people keep enjoying benefits and recognition, is shortsighted. Also, this kind of conclusion might have been made in haste. If one analyzes carefully, one finds that troublemakers are definitely not happy. It is better to behave well and take responsibility for one's actions, and lead a positive life.

APRIL 3

I have found that the greatest degree of inner tranquility comes from the development of love and compassion. The more we care for the happiness of others, the greater is our own sense of well-being. Cultivating a close, warmhearted feeling for others automatically puts the mind at ease. It is the ultimate source of success in life.

It seems to me that Western science and Eastern philosophy can join together to create a really complete and full-fledged human being. It is only in this way that man will emerge strengthened from his condition and become whole. What in fact interests me is what is beyond matter and awareness, what really is important, and what makes us what we are.

APRIL 5

I understand the meaning of one being "open" as being like an open door; it can open very easily, without difficulty. "Free" is also the same. As a result of being free and open, the more you receive new ideas, it makes you want to give out more of your energy. That way, each helps the other. It is very useful, very necessary; especially these days.

APRIL 6

The grosser consciousness depends heavily on particles of matter. The subtler consciousness is more independent—it does not depend so much on the brain. In the Buddha state, the grosser mind completely disappears.

Luminance, radiance, imminence—the three states of subtle mind—all of these disappear in the clear light, the innermost consciousness.

APRIL 7

The Fully Enlightened One said that all he can do is teach us the Dharma, the path to liberation from suffering; it is up to us to put it into practice—he washed his hands of that responsibility!

Bodhicitta is the medicine which revives and gives life to every sentient being who even hears of it. When you engage in fulfilling the needs of others, your own needs are fulfilled as a by-product.

*T*aking your own body and mind as the laboratory, engage in some thoroughgoing research on your own mental functioning, and examine the possibility of making some positive changes within yourself.

Such practices as bodhicitta automatically bring calmness at the time of death. The mind at the time of death is at a very critical period, and if you are able to leave a strong, positive impact at that time, then it will become a very powerful force in continuing a positive experience in the next life.

If in a competitive society you are sincere and honest, in some circumstances people may take advantage of you. If you let someone do so, he or she will be engaging in an unsuitable action and accumulating bad karma that will harm the person in the future. Thus it is permissible, with an altruistic motivation, to take counteraction in order to prevent the other person from having to undergo the effects of this wrong action.

*T*hree qualities enable people to understand the teachings: objectivity, which means an open mind; intelligence, which is the critical faculty to discern the real meaning by checking the teachings of Buddha; and interest and commitment, which means enthusiasm.

APRIL 13

A strong sense of separateness in the past has brought about competition and warring. But now, we are more interdependent. So we need to communicate, hold dialogs, and compromise.

It would be good to have a bullet that searches for and hits the real troublemaker, which is within us.

Whenever Buddhism has taken root in a new land there has always been a certain variation in the style in which it is observed. The Buddha himself taught differently according to the place, the occasion, and the situation of those who were listening to him. So, all of us have a great responsibility to take the essence of Buddhism and put it into practice in our own lives.

Emptiness should be understood in the context of dependent arising and it should evoke a sense of fullness, of things created by causes and conditions. We shouldn't think that the self is something that is originally there and then eliminated in meditation; in fact, it is something that never existed in the first place.

Natural environment sustains the life of all beings universally. Trees are referred to in accounts of the principal events of Buddha's life. His mother leaned against a tree for support as she gave birth to him. He attained enlightenment seated beneath a tree, and finally passed away as trees stood witness overhead.

APRIL 17

Whatever we say, let us speak clearly and to the point, in a voice that is calm and pleasant, unaffected by attachment or hatred. Look kindly at others, thinking: it is thanks to them that I shall attain Buddhahood.

If we are very forbearing, then something we would normally consider very painful will not appear so bad after all. But without patient endurance, even the smallest thing becomes unbearable. A lot depends on our attitude.

One of the things that meditation teaches us, when we slowly descend into ourselves, is that the sense of peace already exists in us. We all have a deep desire for it even if it's often hidden, masked, thwarted.

If we examine human nature carefully, it is good, well disposed, helpful. And it seems to me that nowadays the spirit of harmony is increasing, that our desire to live together calmly is growing stronger and stronger; it's more and more widespread.

It may surprise you, perhaps, but I am not strictly opposed to the spectacle of violence and crime. It all depends on the lessons you draw from it.

A good heart is both important and effective in daily life. If in a small family, even without children, the members have a warm heart for each other, a peaceful atmosphere will be created. However, if one of the persons feels angry, immediately the atmosphere in the house becomes tense. Despite good food or a nice television set, you will lose peace and calm. Thus, things depend more on the mind than on matter.

Matter is important, we must have it and we must use it properly, but in this century we must combine a good brain with a good heart.

All the problems that every individual meets with in everyday life—famine, unemployment, delinquency, insecurity, psychological deviancy, various epidemics, drugs, madness, despair, terrorism—all that is bound up with the widening gap between the people, which, needless to say, can also be found inside the rich countries.

Our ancient experience confirms it at every instant: everything is linked together, everything is inseparable. Consequently the gap has to be reduced.

APRIL 23

The differences in physiology (skin color, slanted eyes, etc.) and culture that appear to separate people, it seems to me, only unify them all the more. The theories of cultural difference that the history of the world has seen are absurd and pernicious. They lead to nothing but bloody impasses.

Today especially, when images from all over the earth are coming our way, our deep unity seems evident to me. Every new institution ought to take this as its point of departure, as its foundation.

If advertising is for a good cause, it is worthwhile. Buddha advertised enlightenment or nirvana. If it is reasonable and beneficial, it is good; but if it is only for profit, cheating, and exploitation, or is misleading, then it is wrong.

APRIL 25

Cultivating inner discipline is a time-consuming process. Having expectations of immediate results is a sign of impatience. Ironically, what the modern man wants is the best, the fastest, the easiest, and, if possible, the cheapest way.

APRIL 26

People who fight with other human beings out of anger, hatred, and strong emotion, even if they gain victory over their enemies in battle, are not in reality true heroes. What they are doing is slaying corpses, because human beings, being transient, will die. Whether or not these enemies die in the battle is another question, but they will die at some point.

So, in reality, they are slaying those already destined to die. The true hero is the one who gains victory over hatred and anger.

*S*amsara—our conditioned existence in the perpetual cycle of habitual tendencies—and nirvana—genuine freedom from such an existence—are nothing but different manifestations of a basic continuum. So this continuity of consciousness is always present. This is the meaning of tantra, or continuity.

If a patient is a believer, terminal illness can be a stepping-stone for personal growth by following one's beliefs. If one is a nonbeliever, then friends need to show a compassionate attitude as far as possible, and share one's problems.

The dying process begins with the dissolution of the elements within the body. It has eight stages, beginning with the dissolution of the earth element, then the water, fire, and wind elements. This is followed by the experience of the next four stages, which are visions in terms of color: appearance of a white vision, increase of the red element, black near-attainment, and the clear light of death.

In meditation, a practitioner is eventually able to experience the dissolution processes.

Nowadays the world is becoming increasingly materialistic, and mankind is reaching toward the very zenith of external progress, driven by an insatiable desire for power and vast possessions. Yet by this vain striving for perfection in a world where everything is relative, they wander ever further away from inward peace and happiness of the mind. This we can all bear witness to, living as we do plagued by unremitting anxiety in this dreadful epoch of mammoth weapons.

It becomes more and more imperative that the life of the spirit be avowed as the only firm basis upon which to establish happiness and peace.

May

MAY 1

The very purpose of religion is to control yourself, not to criticize others. Rather, we must criticize ourselves. How much am I doing about my anger? About my attachment, about my hatred, about my pride, my jealousy? These are the things which we must check in daily life.

MAY 2

We know that to wage a nuclear war today, for example, would be a form of suicide; or that to pollute the air or the oceans in order to achieve some short-term benefit would be to destroy the very basis for our survival.

As individuals and nations are becoming increasingly interdependent, we have no other choice than to develop what I call a sense of universal responsibility.

MAY 3

Happiness is man's prerogative. He seeks it and each man is equally entitled to his pursuits of happiness; no man seeks misery. Justice and equality belong to man's prerogatives too, but these should derive their practice from altruism and should not have been corroded by the stations of power and wealth.

To build such an altruistic motivation so that justice and equality may coexist, the creation of a staunch moral fabric for the social environment is a prerequisite.

MAY 4

Ideals are very important in one's life. Without ideals you cannot move—whether you achieve them or not is immaterial. But one must try and approximate them.

A spoiled child, almost given up by the parents, who suddenly begins to act and behave well, pleases the parents to no end. Similarly, with proper reliance on the spiritual teacher, one can please the teacher and can quickly purify negativities.

*T*he ultimate authority must always rest with the individual's own reason and critical analysis.

We are born and reborn countless number of times, and it is possible that each being has been our parent at one time or another. Therefore, it is likely that all beings in this universe have familial connections.

In the Tibetan medical system disorders of the flesh are related to ignorance, disorders of the bones to anger, and disorders of the blood to attachment.

*S*words can be turned into ploughshares as has been mentioned in the Bible. It is a beautiful image, a weapon transformed into a tool to serve basic human needs, representing an attitude of inner and outer disarmament.

It is often said that you should make a thorough examination of a potential guru, even if it takes twelve years.

The modern economy has no national boundaries. When we talk about ecology or the environment, when we are concerned about the ozone layer—one individual, one society, one country cannot solve these problems. We must work together. Humanity needs more genuine cooperation.

The foundation for the development of good relations with one another is altruism, compassion, and forgiveness.

MAY 12

I myself still occasionally become irritated and angry and use harsh words toward others. Then, a few moments later when the anger has subsided, I feel embarrassed; the negative words are already spoken, and there is no way to take them back.

Although the words have been uttered and the sound of the voice has ceased to exist, their impact still lives on. Hence, the only thing I can do is to go to the person and apologize, isn't that right?

MAY 13

When I doubt that I exist, I pinch myself. Even if our knowledge of the world and of ourselves is illusory, a "not-born," a "not-become" exists. Without it we wouldn't exist. But we exist in a way that is at once relative (to the activity of our mind) and conditioned (by all the other existences).

MAY 14

If we consider material progress, we see that research started by one person can always be continued by another. But this is not possible with spiritual progress.

The realization we talk about in the Buddha-dharma is something that has to be accomplished by the individual. No one else can do it for us.

MAY 15

There is a drunkenness from the power that we give ourselves over things. This drunkenness leads us to stop controlling our appetites. We want more and still more. Instead of quelling the fire, we reignite it. Instead of seeking inner disarmament— the only kind that counts—we multiply our tools of conquest. And we even forget to check whether the fulfillment of our desire is really the one we had wished for.

MAY 16

Good motivation causes good action. The beauty of action is in the method, and Buddhahood is the beauty of result. Generally beauty means something positive, but if you are subjectively too attached to it and handle it wrongly, it can lead to destruction. But then I wonder about the definition of beauty.

Can you consider the art of killing as beauty, especially painless killing? Or the art of warfare—little expense but a huge amount of destruction? Maybe it is considered as beauty.

MAY 17

It is through listening that your mind will turn with faith and devotion, and you will be able to cultivate joy within your mind and make your mind stable. It is through listening that you will be able to cultivate wisdom and be able to remove ignorance. Therefore, it is worthwhile to engage in listening even if it costs your life.

Listening is like a torch that dispels the darkness of ignorance. And if you are able to make your mental continuum wealthy through listening, no one can steal that wealth. It is supreme wealth.

While you are engaging in the practice of giving you should do so with great happiness and radiance on your face. One should practice giving with a smile and with mental uprightness.

Compassion can be roughly defined in terms of a state of mind that is nonviolent and nonharming, or nonaggressive. Because of this there is a danger of confusing compassion with attachment and intimacy.

We have genuine friendship when it is based on true human feeling, a feeling of closeness in which there is a sense of sharing and connectedness. I would call this type of friendship genuine because it is not affected by the increase or decrease of the individual's wealth, status, or power. The factor that sustains that friendship is whether or not the two people have mutual feelings of love and affection.

MAY 21

We should not be too concerned with our fame or what people say about us, either bad or good, because in reality fame could not make any serious difference to one's life. Therefore, we should have our priorities right, and seek what is truly of value, what is truly of meaning to our life, not just mere fame, which is, after all, empty sounds.

Some individuals sacrifice many of their material possessions, wealth, and even their lives to achieve fame. This type of obsession with seeking fame is very childish and is quite foolish.

You should see that all the external dirt and dust around you is basically a manifestation of the faults and stains within your mind. The most important aim is to purge these stains and faults from within your mind. Therefore, as you cleanse the environment, think that you are also purifying your mind.

MAY 23

Many people think that to be patient in bearing loss is a sign of weakness. I think this is a mistake. It is anger that is a sign of weakness, whereas patience is a sign of strength. For example, a person arguing a point based on sound reasoning remains confident and may even smile while proving his case.

On the other hand, if his reasons are unsound and he is about to lose face, he gets angry, loses control, and starts talking nonsense. People rarely get angry if they are confident in what they are doing. Anger comes more easily in moments of confusion.

MAY 24

I used to feel that if I ever gain a state of cessation, I shall really take a good rest. Once we have attained such a state, we could take a good rest and a real holiday, in the true sense of the word. Until we get to such a state, it is foolish for us to be complacent. When we have attained the state of cessation, we have truly reached a very secure ground.

I find that there are two types of fear. In one kind, things are quite delicate, or critical. At such times, I know that I must make a decision, whether I know what to do or not. First, I try to consult with my friends and reflect on it. Then I make a decision and act, and I never have any regret.

Ultimately, this is very much related to motivation. If I have no negative, selfish motivation, deep down I will have no guilty feeling. A second kind of fear is based on imagination. To overcome that, you need calmness so that you can investigate it more closely. When you look into it in detail, your imaginary fear dissipates.

If a person has never encountered love toward himself or herself from any quarter, it is very sad. But if that person can meet even one person who will show unconditional love—simply acceptance and compassion—if he knows that he is an object of someone else's affection and love, it is bound to have an impact, and this will be appreciated. Because there is a seed in himself, this act of love will start to catalyse or ripen that seed.

Crucial to the hermeneutical approach is the Mahayana principle of the four reliances. These are:

(i) reliance on the teaching, not on the teacher;

(ii) reliance on the meaning, not on the words that express it;

(iii) reliance on the definitive meaning, not on the provisional meaning; and

(iv) reliance on the transcendent wisdom of deep experience, not on mere knowledge.

MAY 28

In one sense, we can say it is delusion itself—in the form of the wisdom derived from delusion—that actually destroys the delusions. Similarly it is the blissful experience of emptiness induced by sexual desire that dissolves the force of sexual impulses. This is analogous to the life of wood-born insects: they consume the very wood from which they are born. Such utilization of the path to enlightenment is a unique feature of *tantra.*

MAY 29

I am sometimes asked whether this vow of celibacy is really desirable and indeed whether it is really possible. Suffice to say that its practice is not simply a matter of suppressing sexual desires.

On the contrary, it is necessary to fully accept the existence of these desires and to transcend them by the power of reasoning. When successful, the result on the mind can be very beneficial. The trouble with sexual desire is that it is a blind desire and can only give temporary satisfaction.

Thus, as Nagarjuna said: "When you have an itch, you scratch. But not to itch at all is better than any amount of scratching."

Encountering sufferings will definitely contribute to the elevation of your spiritual practice, provided you are able to transform the calamity and misfortune into the path.

Discipline is a supreme ornament and, whether worn by the old, young, or middle-aged, it gives birth only to happiness. It is perfume *par excellence* and, unlike ordinary perfumes that travel only with the wind, its refreshing aroma travels spontaneously in all directions. A peerless ointment, it brings relief from the hot pains of delusion.

June

When we are able to recognize and forgive ignorant actions done in one's past, we strengthen ourselves and can solve the problems of the present constructively.

JUNE 2

It is necessary to have a combination of hearing, thinking, and meditation. When you start practicing, you should not expect too much. We live in a time of computers and automation, so you may feel that inner development is also an automatic thing for which you press a button and everything changes. It is not so. Inner development is not easy and will take time.

JUNE 3

The main cause of depression is not a lack of material necessities but a deprivation of the affection of others.

JUNE 4

Anger and hatred cannot bring harmony. The noble task of arms control and disarmament cannot be accomplished by confrontation and condemnation. Hostile attitudes only serve to heat up the situation, whereas a true sense of respect gradually cools down what otherwise could become explosive. We must recognize the frequent contradictions between short-term benefit and long-term harm.

JUNE 5

In the meditation of mental quiescence, in the nine states of mind, there is a state where striving must be abandoned; an effortless concentration is necessary at a certain stage. It is effortless: that means your mind becomes very tranquil—with good qualities and its character complete. At that moment, if you make an effort it will disturb the tranquility. So in order to maintain that pure tranquility, effortless effort must be used.

JUNE 6

On one occasion I entered a hospital in Calcutta where they used huge machines; but they failed in their diagnosis. Our Tibetan doctors, without any instruments, touch the wrists, listen to the various pulses, examine the person, and know quite precisely what is wrong. The whole system is really remarkable.

JUNE 7

A very poor, underprivileged person might think that it would be wonderful to have an automobile or a television set, and should he acquire them, at the beginning he would feel very happy. Now if such happiness were something permanent, it would remain forever. But it does not; it goes. After a few months he wants to change the models. The old ones, the same objects, now cause dissatisfaction. This is the nature of change.

We learn from the principle of dependent origination that things and events do not come into being without causes. Suffering and unsatisfactory conditions are caused by our own delusions and the contaminated actions induced by them.

Dreams are an idea of the mind. There are no tangible objects beneath these sole appearances. Similarly, self and others, samsara and nirvana, are designated by the name and the knowledge about them. Thus, there is no inherent existence of any object.

Buddhahood is a state free of all obstructions to knowledge and disturbing emotions. It is the state in which the mind is fully evolved.

JUNE 11

Guilt, as experienced in Western culture, is connected with hopelessness and discouragement and is past-oriented.

Genuine remorse, however, is a healthy state of mind—it is future-oriented, connected with hope, and causes us to act, to change.

JUNE 12

_T_o study a text, we should take into account the circumstances, the situation, the time, the society, and the community where a book was originally written or a teaching taught.

JUNE 13

Some people might ask, if everything is an illusion, what is the use of getting rid of illusory suffering with an antidote that is itself illusory? The answer is that illusory suffering is the result of causes and conditions that are also illusory. Even though pain is illusory, we still suffer from it, and we certainly do not want it.

The same is true of happiness. It is an illusion, but it is still something we want. Thus, illusory antidotes are used to get rid of illusory sufferings, just like a magician uses one magical illusion to counteract another.

What is endeavor? It is finding joy in doing what is good. To do that, it is necessary to remove anything that counteracts it, especially laziness. Related to these is taking undue pleasure in idleness and sleep and being indifferent to samsara as a state of suffering.

JUNE 15

Cloning is an easy, accurate reproduction that implies that we are putting an end to our evolutionary possibilities. We declare that we are perfect, and we stop there. And, on the other hand, if we do attain immortality, that is, if we suppress our death, by the same token we will have to suppress birth, because the earth would become too rapidly overburdened.

One thing can't be doubted, the "possibility of a quality" is within us. It is called *prajna*. We can deny everything, except that we have the possibility of being better. Simply reflect on that.

JUNE 17

In the case of animals, usually from the facial expression one can tell what they are going through, whereas human beings are much more sophisticated. To some extent you can feel it, but often they can be deceptive; for instance, initially they are nice but then they turn out to be bad, whereas in the other case, initially they are horrible but then they turn out to be good and reliable.

JUNE 18

When we encounter some problem and when someone is about to harm us, then immediately we cultivate anger. Anger comes as a helper or assistant because it makes us bold and courageous and we can retaliate and hit back.

When attachment comes, it comes like our best or closest friend. So they are part of our mind, an innate part, and normally we take them for granted and do not bother much about them when they arise within us. Since they come as our friend or helper, therefore, anger and attachment can really deceive us.

Faith dispels doubt and hesitation, it liberates you from suffering and delivers you to the city of peace and happiness. It is faith that removes the mental turbidity and makes your mind clear. Faith reduces your pride and is the root of veneration. It is the supreme lake because you can easily traverse from one stage of the spiritual path to another. It is like your hand, which can gather all the virtuous qualities.

*B*uddha never mentioned that the problems we have encountered are the result of misconstruction of a house or starting a project or work on an inappropriate day or time.

Buddha always talked about the negative experiences as a result of having performed negative actions. So for a good practitioner there is no new year, there is no good day or bad day.

JUNE 21

To remain discouraged is not the way of a human being, we are not birds and animals, so it is not enough for us to simply lament and complain but we should use our intelligence and work hard.

One aspect of compassion is to respect others' rights and to respect others' views. That is the basis of reconciliation. The human spirit of reconciliation based on compassion is working deep down, whether the person really knows it or not.

Our basic human nature is gentleness; therefore, no matter how much we go through violence and other bad things, ultimately the proper solution is to return to human feeling and affection. So affection or compassion is not only a religious matter, but in our day-to-day life it is quite indispensable.

JUNE 23

As far as your personal requirements are concerned, the ideal is to have fewer involvements, fewer obligations, and fewer affairs, business or whatever. However, so far as the interest of the larger community is concerned, you must have as many involvements as possible and as many activities as possible.

JUNE 24

Within oneself, within each single person, one finds many inconsistencies and contradictions. Sometimes the disparity between one's thoughts early and late in the day is so great that one spends all one's energy trying to figure out how it can be resolved. This can lead to headaches.

So naturally, between two persons, between parents and children, between brothers and sisters, there are differences. Conflicts and disagreements are bound to happen.

If so, then how do we deal with them? If we have confidence in our capacity for reconciliation then we will be able to deal with these situations.

When we talk of the six perfections—generosity, ethical discipline, patience, perseverance, concentration, and wisdom—they can also be found in other, non-bodhisattva practitioners who are working more toward their own individual liberation. What makes the practice of these six factors perfect is the motivation involved.

In order for one's practice of patience to be a practice of the perfection of patience, you need the motivation which is bodhicitta. If your practice is motivated by bodhicitta—the aspiration to attain enlightenment for the benefit of all—then your practice becomes truly a practice of perfection.

JUNE 26

Time never waits but keeps flowing. Not only does time flow unhindered, but correspondingly our lives too keep moving onward all the time.

If something goes wrong, we cannot turn back time and try again. In that sense, there is no genuine second chance.

JUNE 27

A single word or expression in tantra can have four different meanings corresponding to the four levels of interpretation, known as the four modes of understanding, which are:

(i) the literal meaning;
(ii) the general meaning;
(iii) the hidden meaning; and
(iv) the ultimate meaning.

JUNE 28

I don't have any experience in applying Western psychotherapy to the Buddhist path. I do know, however, that intimacy is necessary for a spiritual practitioner, especially if that individual is trying to overcome his mental problems.

When you open yourself up mentally, you do so only with someone you trust from the bottom of your heart, someone you feel very close to. To open yourself up in this way is an important step in overcoming mental problems.

The earth is, to a certain extent, our mother. She is so kind, because whatever we do, she tolerates it. But now, the time has come when our power to destroy is so extreme that Mother Earth is compelled to tell us to be careful. The population explosion and many other indicators make that clear, don't they? Nature has its own natural limitations.

JUNE 30

Tranquil or calm abiding is a heightened state of awareness possessing a very single-pointed nature, accompanied by faculties of mental and physical suppleness. Your body and mind become especially flexible, receptive, and serviceable.

Special insight is a heightened state of awareness, also accompanied by mental and physical suppleness, in which your faculty of analysis is immensely advanced. Thus, calm abiding is absorptive in nature, whereas special insight is analytic in nature.

July

JULY 1

Peace is of little value to someone who is dying of hunger or cold. It will not remove the pain of torture inflicted on a prisoner of conscience. It does not comfort those who have lost their loved ones in floods caused by senseless deforestation in a neighboring country.

Peace can only last where human rights are respected, where the people are fed, and where individuals and nations are free. True peace with ourselves and with the world around us can only be achieved through the development of mental peace.

JULY 2

*F*irst we must help; then, later we can talk about the causes of any tragedy. There is an Indian saying: if you are struck by a poisonous arrow, it is important first to pull it out. There is no time to ask who shot it, what sort of poison it is, and so on.

First handle the immediate problem, and later investigate. Similarly, when we encounter human suffering, it is important to respond with compassion rather than to question the politics of those we help.

Due to karmic influences, the world appears in different ways to certain people. Like when a human being, a god, and a *preta*—three sentient beings—look at one bowl of water, the karmic factors make the human being see it as water while the god sees nectar and the *preta* sees blood. The same object, due to special forces of karma, appears differently to each of them.

In the correlation between ethics and politics, should deep moral convictions form the guideline for the political practitioner, man and his society will reap far-reaching benefits. It is an absurd assumption that religion and morality have no place in politics and that a man of religion should seclude himself as a hermit.

JULY 5

I believe in justice and in human determination. In the history of man it has already been proved that the human will is more powerful than the gun. So although for us this is the toughest period, I quite firmly believe that the Tibetan people, their culture, and the Tibetan faith will survive, will flourish once again.

JULY 6

Human relations based on mutual compassion and love are fundamentally important to human happiness.

JULY 7

Rather than being unhappy and hateful, we should rejoice in the success of others.

Unlike an external enemy, the inner enemy cannot regroup and launch a comeback once it has been destroyed from within.

There are many circumstances that make us unjust, ambitious, or aggressive. All around us, everything is pushing us in that direction, often out of some commercial interest: I have to possess this or that object; otherwise, my life will be lamentable.

The world is presented to us as essentially competitive, divided into "the winners" and "the losers," but that too is a false vision, deliberately false. It is a rapid scan of the surface, which eliminates any descent into the self, any meditation and reflection.

The power of media, whether direct or indirect, is a real power which acts on us, which modifies our behavior, our tastes, and probably our thoughts. Like all authority, it cannot be applied at random. Otherwise, that power could become arbitrary and irresponsible.

The power gives mediamen responsibility comparable to religious or political responsibility. In their own way they contribute to the establishment and maintenance of a human community. The well-being of that community should be their first concern.

JULY 11

The training of the mind is an art. If this can be considered as art, one's life is art. I am not interested in the physical aspect of art. I simply meditate and train my mind. And as far as external appearance is concerned, nature in its pristine form is also art.

If you rely on someone who has lower qualities than yourself, that will lead to your degeneration; if you rely on someone who has qualities similar to yourself, you will stay where you are; and if you rely on someone who has better qualities than yourself, that will help you to achieve sublime status.

JULY 13

I sometimes think that the act of bring-
ing food is one of the basic roots of all
relationships.

JULY 14

If students sincerely point out the faults of the guru and explain any contradictory behavior, this will, in fact, help the guru to correct that behavior and adjust any wrong actions.

JULY 15

For a meditator who has a certain degree of inner stability and realization, every experience comes as a teaching; every event, every experience one is exposed to comes as a kind of learning experience.

When a problem first arises, try to remain humble, maintain a sincere attitude, and be concerned that the outcome is fair. Of course, others may try to take advantage of you, and if your remaining detached only encourages unjust aggression, adopt a strong stand. This, however, should be done with compassion, and if it is necessary to express your views and take strong countermeasures, do so without anger or ill intent.

There are different types of attachment in relation to different objects: attachment toward form, appearance, sound, smell, tactile sensations, and so on. All of these individually are powerful enough to cause a lot of problems and difficulties. However, the strongest form of attachment seems to be sexual attachment. Here we find attachment toward all the five senses involved. Therefore, it is all the more powerful and has the potential for problems and destruction.

Should we persist in our normal self-centered tendencies and behavior in spite of our human birth, we would be wasting a great opportunity. Our tenure in this world should not be that of a troublemaker in the human community.

Great compassion and wisdom are the chief qualities of the Buddha. Even in worldly terms, the more intelligent and knowledgeable a person is, the more the person commands respect. Similarly, the more compassionate, kind, and gentle a person, the more he or she should be respected.

So if you are able to develop that intelligence and altruism to their fullest extent, then you are truly admirable and deserve to be respected.

Delusion is a state of mind that is very obvious: when it arises within the mind it causes mental disturbances and anxieties in the individual. Furthermore, it causes many problems and difficulties in society, often on a national scale.

Right from the beginning of human civilization, delusions have been the real causes of problems, trouble, and conflict within society. It is delusion that forces one to be attracted and attached to one's own side and to feel hatred and anger toward the opposite side. Thus, one creates many divisions within the human community. All of these come about through the underlying force of the attachment to one's own self.

JULY 21

In the present circumstances, no one can afford to assume that someone else will solve their problems. Every individual has a responsibility to help guide our global family in the right direction. Good wishes are not sufficient; we must become actively engaged.

In the case of making bombs, the people involved are specialists. They are focusing on something very narrow and becoming extremely expert in that area, without seeing the broader consequences of their acts. It is a kind of tunnel vision. As long as they focus on that, the self-deception is supported. From the exploitist's viewpoint, this is a great achievement. In their own right, in their own domain, they are doing something extraordinary.

The guru, the spiritual teacher, is responsible for his or her improper behavior. It is the student's responsibility not to be drawn into it. The blame is on both. Partly it is because the student is too obedient and devoted to the spiritual master—a kind of blind acceptance of that person's guidance. This always spoils the person. But of course part of the blame lies with the spiritual master, because he lacks the integrity that is necessary to be immune to that kind of vulnerability.

When through rituals and formalities you create the spiritual space and atmosphere that you are seeking, then the process will have a powerful effect on your experience. When you lack the inner dimension for that spiritual experience you are aspiring to, then rituals become mere formalities, external elaborations. In that case, clearly, they lose their meaning and become unnecessary customs—just a good excuse for passing time.

*S*exual misconduct has negative spiritual and social consequences. It causes disharmony between life partners and has an adverse effect upon their children. Rape is worse, harming another's body by force, leading justifiably to controversies in courts of law and multiplying social problems.

When others insult, rebuke, and speak unpleasant words to us, although an intolerable pain arises like a thorn at the heart, if we comprehend the teachings then we can recognize the essenceless nature of these words which resemble an echo. So just as when an inanimate object is scolded, we will experience not the slightest mental turmoil.

JULY 27

Today we face a number of problems. Some are natural calamities, which we must accept and face as best as we can. But some others are man-made problems created by our own misbehavior and bad thoughts, which can be avoided.

One such problem arises from ideological or even religious conflicts when men fight each other, losing sight of human ends or goals. All different faiths and systems are only methods to achieve a goal that for the average person is happiness in life.

Therefore, at no time should we place means above ends: the supremacy of man over matter and all that it entails must be maintained at all times.

JULY 28

The fact remains that the birth cycles of all sentient beings are beginningless, and that countless times in previous lives we have each fulfilled the role of a mother. The feeling of a mother for her child is a classic example of love.

For the safety, protection, and welfare of her children, a mother is ready to sacrifice her very life. Recognizing this, children should be grateful to their mothers and express their gratitude by performing virtuous deeds.

JULY 29

One of the characteristics of karmic theory is that there is a definite, commensurate relationship between cause and effect. There is no way that negative actions or unwholesome deeds can result in joy and happiness. Joy and happiness, by definition, are the results or fruits of wholesome actions. So from that point of view, it is possible for us to admire not so much the immediate action, but the real causes of joy.

There is said to be a relationship between dreaming, on the one hand, and the gross and subtle levels of the body on the other. But it's also said there is such a thing as a "special dream state." In that state, the "special dream body" is created from the mind and from vital energy within the body.

This special dream body is able to dissociate entirely from the gross physical body and travel elsewhere. One way of developing this special dream body is first of all to recognize the dream as a dream when it is over. Then you find that the dream is malleable, and you can make efforts to gain control over it.

Regarding my actual daily practice, I spend, at the very least, five and a half hours per day in prayer, meditation, and study. On top of this, I also pray whenever I can during odd moments of the day; for example, over meals and while traveling. In this last case, I have three main reasons for doing so: first, it contributes toward fulfillment of my daily duty; second, it helps to pass the time productively; third, it assuages fear! I see no distinction between religious practice and daily life.

August

AUGUST 1

When we practice, initially, as a basis we control ourselves, stopping the bad actions which hurt others as much as we can. This is defensive. After that, when we develop certain qualifications, then as an active goal we should help others.

In the first stage, sometimes we need isolation; however, after you have some confidence, some strength, you must remain in contact with society, and serve it in any field—health, education, politics, or whatever. In order to serve you must remain in society.

According to its level of subtlety, consciousness is classified into three levels: the waking state or gross level of consciousness; the consciousness of the dream state, which is more subtle; and the consciousness during sleep, dreamless sleep, which is subtler still.

Similarly, the three stages of birth, death, and the intermediate state are also established in terms of the subtlety of their levels of consciousness. On the basis of the continuity of the stream of consciousness is established the existence of rebirth and reincarnation.

We must each lead a way of life with self-awareness and compassion, to do as much as we can.
Then, whatever happens, we will have no regrets.

AUGUST 4

We can speak of an effect and a cause on both the disturbing side and the liberating side. The true sufferings and true causes of sufferings are the effect and cause on the side of things that we do not want; the true cessation and the true paths are the effect and cause on the side of things that we desire.

Vegetarianism is very admirable. However, according to Buddhism, there is no unequivocal prohibition against eating meat. What is specifically prohibited is taking any meat that you have ordered with the knowledge, or even the suspicion, that it has been killed especially for you.

When receiving the teachings, it is important to have the correct attitude. It is not practicing the Dharma properly to listen with the intention of gaining material advantage or reputation. Neither should our goal be higher rebirth in the next life, nor should we be wishing only for our own liberation from samsara. These are all attitudes we should reject. Instead, let us listen to the teachings with the determined wish to attain the state of omniscience for the sake of all beings.

In Tibetan, the word for blessing means "transformation through majesty or power." In short, the meaning of blessing is to bring about, as a result of the experience, a transformation in one's mind for the better.

The truth of suffering is that we experience many different types of suffering. The three categories are: suffering of suffering—this refers to things such as headaches; suffering of change—this is related to the feeling of restlessness after being comfortable; and all-pervasive suffering that acts as the basis of the first two categories and is under the control of karma and the disturbing mind.

AUGUST 9

The criterion that distinguishes a school as Buddhist is its acceptance of four fundamental tenets, known as the four seals. These are:

(i)   all composite phenomena are impermanent;
(ii) all contaminated things and events are unsatisfactory;
(iii) all phenomena are empty and selfless; and
(iv) nirvana is true peace.

*T*rue practitioners are unaffected by external pressures and their own emotions; they are free to secure the temporary and ultimate benefit of both themselves and others. They remain independent, fear nothing, and are never at odds with themselves. Always peaceful, they are friendly with all, and everything they say is helpful.

Wherever we go, let us be humble and avoid being noisy or bossy. Let us not hurt other people's feelings or cause them to act negatively.

When things are not going well for someone we dislike, what is the point in rejoicing? It does not make his present suffering any worse and even if it did, how sad it would be that we should wish such a thing.

Our whole educational system is in a crisis. It can't adapt. In fact, this crisis extends to industry and politics. Everything seems to be escaping our thought, and hence our control.

It seems to me that God has fallen asleep somewhere. I was joking, as you might imagine, since we
make no allowance for a creator god. But it is true
that if God has fallen asleep, then it is our job to
wake Him up. One can't blame all our troubles on
God. Nor on destiny, nor on karma, which is our law
of the chain of causes, of deeds, and effects. All this
comes from a rather cowardly attitude.

I am absolutely opposed to the death penalty. My predecessor abolished it in Tibet. Today I find it unbelievable that it persists in large countries like China and India. They still kill people in the name of justice in the country of Mahatma Gandhi! In the very land where the Buddha taught!

The death penalty is pure violence, a barbaric and useless violence. Dangerous even, because it can only lead to other acts of violence—as all violence does. The supreme punishment ought to be a life sentence, and one without brutality.

AUGUST 15

It is difficult to impose censorship in a democracy. Though we can still see censorship at work in India, real violence and even explicit eroticism are permitted in Indian films. Women can display themselves very provocatively, as they do everywhere else. Yet until recently men and women never kissed on the lips. People killed one another, but they didn't kiss. And yet it is more agreeable to kiss than to kill!

In Indian films, most of the time we witness the development of a love story, which meets violent opposition, but in the end the good-hearted people are reunited and rewarded, while the villains are punished.

In the cycle of rebirths, which we call samsara, from time to time there occurs the phenomenon of reincarnation. First of all, let us make a distinction. The cycle of rebirths—samsara—is the very condition of all life. No existence escapes it, unless it gets to nirvana. This condition is painful, because it obliges us to live and live again, on levels that can be worse than those we have known. If rebirth is an obligation, reincarnation is a choice. It is the power granted to certain worthy individuals to control their future birth.

Guilt, according to some scholars, is something that can be overcome. It does not exist in Buddhist terminology. With the Buddha nature all negative things can be purified. Guilt is incompatible with our thinking as you are part of an action but not fully responsible for it. You are just part of the contributing factor. However, in some cases one must repent, deliberately hold responsibility, have regret, and never commit the mistake again.

If you get proud and haughty as a result of long study and understanding, it is very unfortunate. If we see pride among people who have no idea about Dharma practice, it is understandable. However, if afflictive emotions and haughtiness are present among Dharma practitioners, it is a great disgrace to the practice.

The advantage of relying on a spiritual teacher is that if you have accumulated an action that would project you into a negative state of existence, the result of that could be experienced just in this life in the form of minor sufferings or minor problems, or even experiencing the result in a dream and through that way one could destroy the destructive result of negative actions.

In the case of the death of a person who has been engaging in nonvirtuous practices, the consciousness would start dissolving from the upper part of the body and withdraw within the heart. In the case of a person who has performed virtuous activities, the dissolution of the heat starts from the lower part of the body and finally withdraws at the heart. In both cases the transference of consciousness would take place at the center.

One should enter or perform spiritual practice with a motivation similar to the motivation and attitude of a child who is fully absorbed in sports or play. A child fully engrossed in play gets so delighted with it that the child never feels satisfied—such should be your mental attitude in making effort in Dharma practice.

There are many afflictive emotions such as conceit, arrogance, jealousy, desire, lust, closed-mindedness, and so on, but of all these, hatred or anger is singled out as the greatest evil. This is done for two reasons. One is that hatred or anger is the greatest stumbling block for a practitioner who is aspiring to enhance his or her altruism and attain a good heart. Second, when hatred or anger are generated they have the capacity to destroy one's virtue and calmness of mind.

It is possible to indicate one's particular spiritual way of life through external means, such as wearing certain clothes, having a shrine or altar in one's house, doing recitations and chanting. However, these practices are secondary to one's religious or spiritual way of life because all of these activities can be performed by a person who harbors a very negative state of mind.

On the other hand, all the virtues of mind, the mental qualities, are genuine spiritual qualities because all of these internal mental qualities cannot exist in a single moment simultaneously with ill feelings or negative states of mind.

Regarding intergender relationships, I see two principal types of relationships based on sexual attraction. One form is pure sexual desire in which the motive or impetus is temporary satisfaction, a sort of immediate gratification. But it is not very reliable or stable because the individuals are relating to each other not as people, but rather as objects.

In the second type, attraction is not predominantly physical. Rather, there is an underlying respect and appreciation of the value of the other person, based on one's feeling that the other person is kind, nice, and gentle. One can therefore accord respect and dignity to that other individual.

AUGUST 25

While one possesses the facilities of wealth, position, education, and so on, it is crucial that there be some internal restraining factor that constantly keeps one in check so one is not spoiled by these facilities and never loses the fundamental insight into the underlying unsatisfactory nature of cyclic existence. The proper perspective is to utilize this as an aid in the path, and in working for the benefit of other sentient beings.

There is always the need to maintain balance, not to go to any extremes, and to have full knowledge of how to proceed along the path in the best and most effective way.

*T*here are three types of joyous effort:

(i) armorlike joyous effort;
(ii) joyous effort in gathering virtues; and
(iii) joyous effort in working for others.

The main obstacles to the development of these efforts are the different levels of laziness—primarily the laziness of procrastination, and the laziness stemming from indolence and from a sense of inferiority.

AUGUST 27

In addition to practicing during the waking state, if you can also use your consciousness during sleep for wholesome purposes, then the power of your spiritual practice will be all the greater. Otherwise, at least a few hours each night will be just a waste. So if you can transform your sleep into something virtuous, this is useful. The *Sutrayana* method is to try as you go to sleep to develop a wholesome mental state, such as compassion, or the visualization of impermanence or emptiness.

The creatures that inhabit this earth—be they human beings or animals—are here to contribute, each in its own particular way, to the beauty and prosperity of the world. Many creatures have toiled singly or jointly to make our lives comfortable. The food we eat, the clothes we wear, have not just dropped from the sky. Many creatures have labored to produce them. That is why we should be grateful to all our fellow creatures.

Compassion and loving kindness are the hallmarks of achievement and happiness.

Overall I have found much that is impressive about Western society. In particular, I admire its energy and creativity and hunger for knowledge.

On the other hand, a number of things about the Western way of life cause me concern. People there have an inclination to think in terms of "black and white," and "either, or," which ignores the facts of interdependence and relativity.

Between two points of view they tend to lose sight of the gray areas. Also, with thousands of brothers and sisters for neighbors, so many people appear to be able to show their true feelings only to their cats and dogs.

Blessings are not enough. Blessings must come from within. Without your own effort, it is impossible for blessings to come.

A skilled physician ministers to his patients individually, giving each the appropriate medicine necessary to cure his particular disease. Furthermore, the method and materials of treatment will vary according to the particular combination of circumstances of time and country. Yet all the widely differing medicines and medical methods are similar in that each of them aims to deliver the suffering patient from his sickness.

In the same way, all religious teachings and methods are intended to free living beings from misery and the cause of misery and to provide them with happiness and the cause of happiness.

September

The task of man is to help others; that's my firm teaching, that's my message. That is my own belief. For me, the fundamental question is better relations; better relations among human beings—and whatever I can contribute to that.

One great question underlies our experience, whether we think about it consciously or not: what is the purpose of life? From the moment of birth, every human being wants happiness and does not want suffering. Neither social conditioning nor education nor ideology affects this. From the very core of our being, we simply desire contentment. Therefore, it is important to discover what will bring about the greatest degree of happiness.

A limit to the size of the family is desirable. We have to take care of birth control. It is very, very essential to have fewer children, and those children must be properly taken care of. Besides education, one must introduce to them the reverence for life and the value of human affection.

To overcome attachment we should meditate on the ugliness of what attracts us. The antidote to pride is meditation on the aggregates. To counteract ignorance we should concentrate on the movement of the breath and on interdependence.

The root of the mind's turmoil is, in fact, ignorance on account of which we fail to understand the true nature of things. The mind is brought under control by purifying our mistaken notion of reality.

The three physical nonvirtues are killing, stealing, and sexual misconduct.

The four verbal nonvirtues are lying, divisiveness, harsh speech, and senseless speech.

The three mental nonvirtues are covetousness, harmful intent, and wrong view.

Perhaps in monasteries in the West there is leisure, but outside—especially in the cities—life seems to be running at a rapid pace, like a clock, never stopping for an instant! So if you look at life in an urban community, it seems as if every aspect of a person's life has to be so precise, designed like a screw that has to fit exactly in the hole.

In some sense, you have no control over your own life. In order to survive, you have to follow this pattern and the pace that is set for you.

Just like the earth, may I support beings as numerous as the sky is vast. And as long as they have not attained enlightenment, may I devote myself entirely to their happiness.

When people get angry they lose all sense of happiness. Even if they are good-looking and normally peaceful, their faces turn livid and ugly. Anger upsets their physical well-being and disturbs their rest; it destroys their appetites and makes them age prematurely. Happiness, peace, and sleep evade them, and they no longer appreciate people who have helped them and deserve their trust and gratitude.

Leaving aside memory—which allows us to remember, for example, the experiences of our youth—we all have latent and unconscious tendencies that arise under certain circumstances and influence the way our minds react. Such tendencies are the product of powerful experiences in the recent or distant past, which cause us to react unconsciously without our necessarily remembering those experiences.

It is difficult to explain these tendencies and how they manifest other than by saying that they are the imprints of past experiences on the subtle consciousness.

The growth in population is very much bound up with poverty, and in turn poverty plunders the earth. When human groups are dying of hunger, they eat everything; grass, insects, everything. They cut down the trees, they leave the land dry and bare. All other concerns vanish. That's why in the next thirty years the problems we call "environmental" will be the hardest that humanity has to face.

Since we have a natural compassion in us, and that compassion has to manifest itself, it might be good to awaken it. Violence done to an innocent person, for example, can make us indignant, scandalize us, and in so doing help us to discover our compassion. By its very violence, television might keep us in a state of alert. However, it is very dangerous if violence leads to indifference. Thus, a central point of our teaching is how to reach nonattachment without falling into indifference.

SEPTEMBER 12

A real "Tibethood" was born from the difficult passage in the long history of Tibet. Centuries and centuries of rootedness can make you forget that feeling. The bonds with the earth seem secure, untouchable. Then something unexpected happens that calls those bonds into question. You discover a cynical brutality, the crushing use of force, your own weakness.

Finally, you leave, you never see your country except from far away. It gets ravaged, occupied, and still you realize that it hasn't disappeared, that it subsists in you, that you still feel Tibetan. Then you begin to wonder, what does being Tibetan mean?

We are afraid to die because we don't know the day nor the hour, because death can surprise us at any moment. Because we fear what comes after death, we are afraid of finding ourselves in an unknown and disagreeable place, filled with anxiety. If we want to die well, we must learn to live well.

The experience of death is extremely important, because our state of mind at that moment can decide the quality of our future rebirth. We can even, at the moment of dying, make a special effort. In the course of it meditation can reach an unequalled summit, as shown by the preservation of the body.

Just as rust, which arose from the iron itself, wears out the iron, likewise, performing an action without examination would destroy us by projecting us into a negative state of existence.

SEPTEMBER 15

As students, you should first watch and investigate thoroughly. Do not consider someone as a teacher or guru until you have certain confidence in the person's integrity. This is very important. Even after that, if some unhealthy things happen, you have the liberty to reject them. Students should make sure that they don't spoil the guru.

There are three types of wisdom, or three stages in one's understanding. First is the stage of hearing or learning, the initial stage when you read or hear about something.

The second stage is when, after learning, you think about the issue or the topic constantly, and through constant familiarity and thinking, your understanding becomes clearer. Then at that time you begin to have certain feelings or experiences.

This third stage is called "meditatively acquired wisdom." This is when you not only intellectually understand the subject matter but also, through meditative experience, are able to feel it.

It is vital for a leader to keep in touch with the common people. I myself had learned at an early age that anyone who wishes to lead must remain close to the common people.

Our judgements, even concerning ordinary things, are frequently clouded by our emotions. For example, we often see the actions of our loved ones—even if they are harmful—as wonderful, whereas we judge even the positive actions of a person we dislike as pretentious and false.

We cannot rely upon our perceptions; it is a fact that we misapprehend many situations. If this is a general fact, how can we still stubbornly maintain that our perceptions about our own spiritual masters must be true?

Human beings are social animals who depend for their survival on others' cooperation and assistance. So it is better not to have a companion at all than to have one who is very aggressive and harmful. You can never rely on such a person but always have to be suspicious and apprehensive about him or her.

Conversely, if your own character and personality is such that all people avoid you, that is very sad. Therefore, a kind heart and compassion are the real sources of peace and happiness.

Whether their entire life will be successful or not depends much upon the atmosphere young children feel throughout the day. In a family where there is love and compassion, the children will become happier and more successful human beings. Without love, there is a danger of spoiling or ruining their whole life. Human affection is thus most influential for children's development.

Western brains work, they work a great deal, but always in the direction of efficiency. In that way the mind puts itself at the service of the result. Like all servants, it renounces its independence. I am talking about another form of spiritual life, more detached and deeper, free from the obsession of a goal to be reached. In a way, the universal invasion of technology, everywhere it goes, lessens the life of the mind.

If you are the sort of person who always speaks nicely in front of others but says nasty things about them behind their backs, of course nobody will like you.

There is no way to escape death, it is just like trying to escape when you are surrounded by four great mountains touching the sky. There is no escape from these four mountains of birth, old age, sickness, and death. Aging destroys youth, sickness destroys health, degeneration of life destroys all excellent qualities, and death destroys life.

Even if you are a great runner, you cannot run away from death. You cannot stop death with your wealth, through your magic performances or recitation of mantras, or even your medicines. Therefore, it is wise to prepare for your death.

There is a true feminist movement in Buddhism that relates to the goddess Tara. Following her cultivation of bodhicitta, the bodhisattva's motivation, she looked on those striving toward full awakening and she felt that there were too few people who attained Buddhahood as women. So she vowed, "I have developed bodhicitta as a woman. For all of my lifetimes along the path I vow to be born as a woman, and in my final lifetime when I attain Buddhahood, then, too, I will be a woman."

Anything that contradicts experience
and logic should be abandoned.

The metaphor of light is a common image in all the major religious traditions. In the Buddhist context, light is particularly associated with wisdom and knowledge; darkness is associated with ignorance and a state of misknowledge.

This corresponds to the two aspects of the path: there is the method aspect, which includes such practices as compassion and tolerance, and the wisdom or knowledge aspect, the insight penetrating the nature of reality.

It is the knowledge or wisdom aspect of the path that is the true antidote to dispelling ignorance.

We do not regard a person as an authority simply on the basis of their fame, position, power, good looks, wealth, and so on, but rather because we find what they say on issues related to their particular field of expertise convincing and reliable.

In brief, we do not generally take a person to be an authority on a subject simply out of respect and admiration for them as a person. Similarly, when we take the Buddha as an authority, as a reliable teacher, we do so on the basis of having investigated and examined his principal teaching, the Four Noble Truths.

SEPTEMBER 28

I am talking to you and you are listening to me. We are generally under the impression that there is a speaker and an audience and there is the sound of words being spoken but, in ultimate truth, if I search within myself I will not find the words, and if you search yourselves you will not find them—they are all void like empty space. Yet they are not completely nonexistent. They must exist, for we are able to feel them.

What I am saying is being heard by you, and you are in turn thinking on the subject. My speech is producing some effects, yet if we search for them we cannot find them. This mystery relates to the dual nature of truth.

I find that giving a discourse based on religious texts is a good way of showing that religion has a lot to tell us, no matter what situation we find ourselves in. However, I am better at it now than I was in the beginning. In those days I lacked confidence, although it improved every time I spoke in public. Also, I found, as every teacher does, that there is nothing like teaching to help one learn.

Our experience is based on the five inner and five outer elements. When your meditative experience gets deep enough to control the five inner elements, then there is the possibility of controlling the five outer elements.

Although space seems empty, once you develop the energies, you can control it. When that happens, you can look right through solid things and walk in empty space as if it were solid.

October

Man and society are interdependent, hence the quality of man's behavior as an individual and as a participant in his society is inseparable. Reparations have been attempted in the past in order to lessen the malaise and dysfunctional attitudes of our social world in order to build a society that is more just and equal.

Institutions and organizations have been established with their charters of noble ideology to combat these social problems. For all intents and purposes, the objectives have been laudable; but it has been unfortunate that basically good ideas have been defeated by man's inherent self-interest.

An area in Tibetan Buddhism which may be of interest to scientists is the relationship between the physical elements and the nerves, in particular the relationship between the elements in the brain and consciousness.

Involved here are the changes in consciousness, happy or unhappy states of mind etc., the kind of effect they have on the elements within the brain, and the consequent effect that it has on the body. Certain physical illnesses, for example, improve or worsen according to the state of mind.

All the waters and rivers of different lands and climes have their ultimate meeting point in the ocean. So, too, the differing viewpoints on society, the variety of economic theories, and the means to their attainment benefit mankind itself.

There is no point in indulging in dissension-creating discussions on differing ideologies. No positive result has accrued from attempting to convert all men of different temperaments and likings into one common ideology and mode of behavior. This can clearly be seen from the contemporary history of both the East and the West.

Make efforts to consider as transitory all adverse circumstances and disturbances. Like ripples in a pool, they occur and soon disappear. Insofar as our lives are karmically conditioned, they are characterized by endless cycles of problems. One problem appears and passes, and soon another one begins.

Buddha advises, "O *bhikshus* and wise men, just as a goldsmith would test his gold by burning, cutting, and rubbing it, so must you examine my words and accept them but not merely out of reverence for me."

Wise parents, without any anger, may sometimes scold or even punish their children. This is permissible, but if you really get angry and whack the child too much, then you will feel regret in the future. However, with a good motivation of seeking a child's welfare, it is possible to display an expression appropriate to what the child needs at that moment.

The ignorance, arrogance, and obstinacy of certain individuals, whether their intentions were good or evil, have been at the root of all the tragedies of history. The mere names of these ruthless tyrants inspire fear and loathing. So the extent to which people will like us naturally depends on how much, or how little, we think of others' good.

Exile has helped me. When, at some point in our lives, we meet a real tragedy—which could happen to any one of us—we can react in two ways. Obviously, we can lose hope, let ourselves slip into discouragement, into alcohol, drugs, and unending sadness. Or else we can wake ourselves up, discover in ourselves an energy that was hidden there, and act with more clarity, more force.

OCTOBER 9

The void, shunyata, among the four fundamental Buddhist notions (the three others being impermanence, interdependence, and suffering) is certainly the most mysterious and hard to grasp. What is this immense edifice of experience and thought that in the end only opens up on an absence of substance? What would be the foundation of that edifice and of the mind that built it?

If the void is the only reality that isn't illusory, who escapes the net of all maya? Who has cast this net? Can one live over a dizzying void? Can we imagine a dream without a dreamer? The void is a scientific notion. We are empty; the matter that composes us is, so to speak, empty.

Another issue which is very dear to my vision of the future is global demilitarization. This may sound idealistic to many people. I am aware that implementing it requires a step-by-step approach that will entail a process of rethinking in policy and public education.

The first step toward this goal is an international ban on the arms trade and an expansion of demilitarized zones in all parts of the world. Recent progress on dismantling nuclear arsenals and nuclear test bans represent an encouraging and significant beginning.

In the case of a small child, the child has to grow up into a well-built young man, but the growth takes place with the passage of time. It cannot happen overnight. Likewise the transformation of mind will also take time. Nowadays in many places, by using certain injections, pigs, cows, and birds suddenly grow. Then they are killed and consumed. This negative practice also has an effect on human beings. So, when we talk of spiritual practice, we cannot inject certain qualities and suddenly transform the mind.

In the beginning of Buddhist practice, our ability to serve others is limited. The emphasis is on healing ourselves, transforming our minds and hearts. But as we continue, we become stronger and increasingly able to serve others. But until then, we may get overwhelmed by the sufferings and difficulties of other people. We may become exhausted and not able to serve others, not to mention ourselves, effectively. It is natural to feel some limitation with both, and we just have to accept that.

When one is in an intense state of hatred, even a very close friend appears somehow "frosty," cold and distant, or quite annoying. If one harbors hateful thoughts, it ruins one's health. Even if one has wonderful possessions, in the moment of anger one feels like throwing them or breaking them. So there is no guarantee that wealth alone can give one the joy or fulfillment that one seeks.

In Buddha's time there was a king who committed the heinous crime of murdering his father. But he was totally overwhelmed by his crime, and depressed. When Buddha visited him he made a statement that parents are to be killed, but he didn't mean it literally. Buddha was using parents as a kind of metaphor for desire and attachment that lead to rebirth.

Because karma and desire combine to create rebirth, in some sense they are like parents. Thus, he meant that karma and desire are to be eliminated.

When one meditates on mindfulness of the body, reflecting upon the manner in which the body comes into being, and examining the causal conditions, then one will also see the impurities of the body. Then from that perspective, one will find that even those who seem successful in worldly terms are not really objects worthy of envy; they are still within the bondage of suffering and dissatisfaction.

The greater the success one enjoys in worldly terms, the more complex the psychological make-up seems to be, because there is a much more complex nexus of hopes and fears, apprehensions and inhibitions.

Negative actions have the potential to increase, whereas positive actions can be destroyed by many adverse circumstances.

There is no possibility of happiness and peace while someone is under the leadership of a very negative person. Therefore, reflect upon the fact that you are under the rule of ignorance; ignorance is like a despotic king, and anger and attachment are like his ministers. We live under the tyranny and influence of ignorance, the self-grasping attitude, and also the self-cherishing attitude—factors that all the buddhas and bodhisattvas treat as real enemies.

There are different types of patience: the patience of being indifferent to the harm inflicted by others, the patience of voluntarily accepting hardship, and the patience developed through reasoned conviction in the Dharma.

Only a spontaneous feeling of empathy with others can really inspire us to act on their behalf. Nevertheless, compassion does not arise mechanically. Such a sincere feeling must grow gradually, cultivated within each individual, based on their own conviction of its worth. Adopting a kind attitude thus becomes a personal matter. How each of us behaves in daily life is, after all, the real test of compassion.

I feel there is a difference between the mental conflicts that one feels and the emotions they give rise to—anger, hostility, and so forth. If you are not able to express the mental conflicts that you have, then at a later point of your life when you are able to express these mental conflicts, they are automatically accompanied by hostility and anger. Therefore, it is important to express one's suffering, not so much the hostility, but rather the suffering.

Great vigilance must be maintained at all times when dealing in areas about which we do not have great understanding. This, of course, is where science can help. We consider things to be mysterious only when we do not understand them.

I realize that results of inquiries are dependent on the experiments employed to achieve them. However, not finding something does not mean that it does not exist. It only proves that the experiment was incapable of finding it. It is also important to keep in mind the limitations imposed by nature itself.

If any sensible person thinks deeply, he will respect justice. There is an inborn appreciation and respect for justice within our human body. In children, we find what is natural to the human character. But as they grow up, they develop a lot of conditioning and wrong attitudes. I often feel there is more truthfulness in a small child and I find many reasons to have confidence in human courage and human nature.

OCTOBER 23

What is reborn are our habits. Enlightenment is the ending of rebirth, which means a complete non-attachment or nonidentification with all thoughts, feelings, perceptions, physical sensations, and ideas.

We speak of three different types of faith. The first is faith in the form of admiration that you have toward a particular person or a particular state of being. The second is aspiring faith. There is a sense of emulation—you aspire to attain that state of being. The third type is the faith of conviction.

As a spiritual trainee, you must be prepared to endure the hardships involved in a genuine spiritual pursuit and be determined to sustain your effort and will. You must anticipate the multiple obstacles that you are bound to encounter along the path and understand that the key to a successful practice is never to lose your determination. Such a resolute approach is very important.

The story of the Buddha's personal life is the story of someone who attained full enlightenment through hard work and unwavering dedication.

If people everywhere are not allowed to strive for the happiness they instinctively want, then they will be dissatisfied and will make problems for everyone. Unless we can create an atmosphere of genuine cooperation—cooperation not gained by threat or force but by heartfelt understanding—life will become ever more difficult. If we can satisfy people at a heart level, peace will ensue. Without the basis of coexistence, if undesirable social, political, and cultural forms continue to be imposed upon people, peace becomes difficult.

Stealing harms others' property and welfare, and disturbs their peace and happiness. When a house is built, an ugly screen and iron bars are put on the windows to protect what is inside from thieves. Have you ever thought how just the sight of those bars, that screen, makes us uneasy and steals some of our peace and happiness?

By maintaining sharp awareness of the function of religion as expressed in the actuality of all teachings, we can escape the ruinous error of sectarian discrimination and partisanship, and we can avoid the grave sin of casting aside any religious teaching.

If there is love, there is hope to have real families, real brotherhood, real equanimity, real peace. If the love within your mind is lost, if you continue to see other beings as enemies, then no matter how much knowledge or education you have, no matter how much material progress is made, only suffering and confusion will ensue.

Human beings will continue to deceive and overpower one another. Basically, everyone exists in the very nature of suffering, so to abuse or mistreat each other is futile. The foundation of all spiritual practice is love. That you practice this well is my only request.

When a day seems to be long, idle gossip makes our day seem shorter. But it is one of the worst ways in which we waste our time. If a tailor just holds the needle in his hand and goes on talking to a customer, the tailoring does not get finished. Besides, the needle might prick his finger. In short, meaningless gossip prevents us from doing any kind of work.

We eschew the path of mundane power, for the healing power of the spirit naturally follows the path of the spirit; it abides not in the stone of fine buildings, nor in the gold of images, nor in the silk from which robes are fashioned, nor even in the paper of holy writ, but in the ineffable substance of the mind and the heart of man. We are free to follow its dictates as laid down by the great teachers—to sublimate our heart's instincts and purify our thoughts.

Through actual practice in his daily life, man well fulfills the aim of all religion, whatever his denomination.

November

Regardless of race, creed, ideology, political bloc (East and West), or economic region (North and South), the most important and basic aspect of all people is their shared humanity—the fact that each person, old, young, rich, poor, educated, uneducated, male, or female, is a human.

This shared humanness and thus the shared aspiration of gaining happiness and avoiding suffering as well as the basic right to bring these about are of prime importance.

Oppression has never, anywhere, succeeded in suppressing the eternal desire of people to live as free men—free to think their own thoughts, free to act as they consider best for the common welfare and live as human beings—not as robots or slaves.

Even if the Chinese leave nothing but ashes in our sacred land, Tibet will rise from these ashes as a free country even if it takes a long time to do so. No imperialist power has succeeded in keeping other people in colonial subjection for long.

It is most unlikely that we shall actually be able to take on the sufferings of others and give them our happiness. When such transference between beings does occur it is the result of some very strong unbroken karmic connection from the past.

The practice of morality, which means guarding your three doors of body, speech, and mind from indulging in unwholesome activities, equips you with mindfulness and conscientiousness. Therefore, morality is the foundation of the Buddhist path.

Our intention should not be spoiled by the eight worldly preoccupations: gain or loss, pleasure or pain, praise or criticism, and fame or infamy.

Nothing is more important than guarding the mind. Let us constantly keep watch over the wild elephant of the mind, curbing it with mindfulness and vigilance. This is how one can avoid being influenced by different external conditions. But even in retreat in a very secluded place, if the mind is not kept under control, it will wander all over the place. Even when completely alone, we can have an enormous amount of negative emotions.

We have been and are still going through end-less suffering without deriving any benefit what-ever from it. Now that we have promised to be good-hearted, we should try not to get angry when others insult us. Being patient might not be easy. It requires considerable concentration. But the result we achieve by enduring these difficulties will be sublime. That is something to be happy about!

NOVEMBER 8

Aggression is an intimate part of ourselves. That is why we have to struggle. Men raised in a strictly nonviolent environment have managed to become the most horrible butchers. This proves that the most insane aggressiveness continues to live in the depths of us. But our true nature is calm.

We all know that the human mind is agitated, subject to frightful jolts. But this agitation isn't the dominant force. It is possible and necessary to master it.

Can the mind even see the mind? We have to answer yes and no. No, because the mind can't be a subject and object at the same time. The mind interferes, whether it wants to or not, whether it knows it or not, in all that it observes; and with all the more reason when it is a question of itself. But the mind cannot see itself completely. However, the principal tool for purifying the mind is the mind itself. The mind is its own creator, at every instant. Hence its responsibility, which is essential.

Longing for eternity exists because we cherish ourselves, provided our daily life is happy. But if it is miserable, then you want to shorten life.

I believe that to meet the challenge of the next century all human beings will have to develop a greater sense of universal responsibility. Each of us must learn to work not just for his or her own self, family, or nation, but for the benefit of all mankind.

It is very old-fashioned to think in terms of my nation, or my country. Universal responsibility is the real key to human survival. Large human movements spring from individual initiatives. Thus it is the individual working for the common welfare who makes the difference.

The countless stars and constellations that we see today were gradually formed and discovered, but the interesting thing is that the more powerful telescopes we use, the more we will find—more and more stars and lives. Thus, the more we have power to see things, the more there is to see.

NOVEMBER 13

A person who knows a lot but does not practice is like a shepherd who does not own any cattle but always looks after a flock of sheep or cattle. Therefore, studying, reflecting, and meditating on the nature of reality is of great significance for the progress of a spiritual practitioner.

*S*peech and bodily activities which accompany mental process must not be allowed to run on in an indiscreet, unbridled, random way. Just as a trainer disciplines and calms a wild and willful steed by subjecting it to skillful and prolonged training, so must the wild, wandering, random activities of body and speech be tamed to make them docile, righteous, and skillful. Therefore, the teachings of Lord Buddha comprise three graded categories for disciplining the mind: *shila* (training in higher conduct); *samadhi* (training in higher meditation); and *prajna* (training in higher wisdom).

To be angry at hearing other people speaking highly of one's enemies is totally inappropriate, because at least in the mind of the person who is praising this enemy, there is some sense of fulfillment, some satisfaction. That person is doing so because he or she feels joyous and happy, and one should rejoice in that because one's enemy has caused someone to be satisfied. If possible one should also join in the praise rather than trying to obstruct it.

There are two types of prayer. Prayers are, for the most part, simply reminders in your daily practice. So, the verses look like prayers but are actually reminders of how to speak, how to deal with problems and other people, etc. In my own daily practice, prayer takes about four hours.

My practice is reviewing compassion, forgiveness, and *shunyata*. Then the major portion is the visualization of deity, mandala, and attendant tantric practice including visualization of death and rebirth. In my case, it is done eight times. So eight times death is eight times rebirth. I am supposed to be preparing for my death. When actual death comes, whether I will succeed or not, I don't know.

In modern scientific terms, physicists, in their pursuit of understanding the nature of physical reality, have reached a stage where they have lost the concept of solid matter; they can't come up with the real identity of matter. So they are beginning to see things in more holistic terms, in terms of interrelationships rather than discreet, independent, concrete objects.

Occasionally people who do not have a proper knowledge of karmic law say that such and such person is very kind and religious, but he always has problems, whereas so and so is very deceptive and negative, but always seems very successful. Such people may think that there is no karmic law at all.

There are others who got to the other extreme and become superstitious, thinking that when someone experiences illness, it is all due to harmful spirits. However, there is a definite relation between causes and effects: that actions not committed will never produce an effect; and that once committed, actions will never lose their potentiality.

Generosity is of three types: giving material aid, giving Dharma, and protecting from fear. "Giving Dharma" refers to the giving of teachings to other sentient beings with pure motivation to benefit them.

When we pray together, I feel something, I do not know whether you would call it blessings, or grace—but in any case there is a certain feeling that we can experience. If we utilize it properly, this feeling is very helpful for developing our inner strength.

In dealing with those who are undergoing great suffering, if you feel "burnout" setting in, if you feel demoralized and exhausted, it is best, for the sake of everyone, to withdraw and restore yourself. The point is to have a long-term perspective.

Look at one person who annoys you, and use the opportunity to counter your own anger and cultivate compassion. But if the annoyance is too powerful—if you find the person so repulsive that you cannot bear to be in his or her presence—it may be better to look for the exit! Here is the principle: It is better not to avoid events or persons who annoy you, who give rise to anger, if your anger is not too strong. But if the encounter is not possible, work on your anger and develop compassion by yourself.

The mind can and must transform itself. It can get rid of the impurities that contaminate it, and rise to the highest level. We all start off with the same capacities, but some people develop them, and others don't. We get very easily used to the mind's laziness, all the more easily because laziness hides beneath the appearance of activity: we run right and left, we make calculations and phone calls. But these activities engage only the most elementary and coarse levels of the mind. They hide the essential from us.

We are all here on this planet, as it were, as tourists. None of us can live here forever. The longest we might live is a hundred years. So while we are here we should try to have a good heart and to make something positive and useful of our lives.

Whether we live just a few years or a whole century, it would be truly regrettable and sad if we were to spend that time aggravating the problems that afflict other people, animals, and the environment. The most important thing is to be a good human being.

Buddha is the teacher, Dharma is the actual refuge, and the *Sangha* is the one which assists in understanding or establishing the objects of refuge.

Ordinary compassion and love give rise to a very close feeling, but it is essentially attachment. As long as the other person appears to you as beautiful or good, love remains, but as soon as he or she appears to you as less beautiful or good, your love completely changes. Even though your dear friend is the same person, he feels more like an enemy. Instead of love, you now feel hostility.

With genuine love and compassion, another person's appearance or behavior has no effect on your attitude. Real compassion comes from seeing the other's suffering. You feel a sense of responsibility, and you want to do something for him or her.

If we examine ourselves every day with mindfulness and mental alertness, checking our thoughts, motivations, and their manifestations in external behavior, a possibility for change and self-improvement can open within us. Although I myself cannot claim with confidence to have made any remarkable progress over the years, my desire and determination to change and improve is always firm.

From early morning until I go to bed and in all situations of life, I always try to check my motivation and be mindful and present in the moment. Personally, I find this to be very helpful in my own life.

Do your best and do it according to your own inner standard (call it conscience), not just according to society's knowledge and judgement of your deeds. "To do our best" is just a phrase of a few words, but it means that at all times in our everyday life we should check our mind so that we don't feel guilty about our mistakes, even though others don't know about it. If we do that, we are doing our best.

It is important to think very well before entering a particular spiritual tradition. Once you have entered you should stick to it. Do not be like a man who tastes food in all the different restaurants but never actually gets down to eating a meal. Think carefully before adopting a practice; then follow it through. This way you will get some results from dedicating even a little time each day. Alternatively, if you try to follow all the various paths you will not get anywhere.

It seems that when men become desperate they consult the gods. And when the gods become desperate, they tell lies!

December

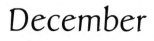

DECEMBER 1

*I*rrespective of whether we are believers or agnostics, whether we believe in God or karma, moral ethics is a code which everyone is able to pursue. We need human qualities such as moral scruples, compassion, and humility. Because of our innate human frailty and weakness, these qualities are only accessible through forceful individual development in a conducive social milieu, so that a more humane world will come into being.

I am always quite cheerful! It is, I think, the result of my own practice and training. In my lifetime, I have lost my country and have been reduced to being totally dependent on the goodwill of others.

I have also lost my mother, and most of my tutors and gurus have passed away, although I now have a few new gurus. Of course these are tragic incidents, and I feel sad when I think about them. However, I don't feel overwhelmed by sadness. Old, familiar faces disappear, and new faces appear, but I still maintain my happiness and peace of mind.

DECEMBER 3

If a person has a really deep interest in spiritual growth, he or she cannot do away with the practice of meditation. That is the key! Just a mere prayer or wish will not affect this inner spiritual change.

The only way for development is through a constant effort through meditation. Of course, in the beginning it is not easy. You may find difficulties, or a loss of enthusiasm. Or perhaps in the beginning there will be too much enthusiasm—then after a few weeks or months, your enthusiasm may wane. We need to develop a constant, persistent approach based on a long-term commitment.

When we talk about violence, we must understand that we are speaking about a phenomenon in which it is almost impossible to predict the outcome. Even though the motivation on the part of the perpetrator of the act may be pure and positive, when violence is used as a means, it is very difficult to predict the consequences. For this reason, it is always better to avoid a situation that may require violent means. However, tolerance and patience do not imply submission or giving in to injustice.

The person who has a tremendous reserve of patience and tolerance has a certain degree of tranquility and calmness in his or her life. Such a person is not only happy and more emotionally grounded, but also seems to be physically healthier and to experience less illness. The person possesses a strong will, has a good appetite, and can sleep with a clear conscience.

If you help others with sincere motivation and sincere concern, that will bring you more fortune, more friends, more smiles, and more success. If you forget about others' rights and neglect others' welfare, ultimately you will be very lonely.

DECEMBER 7

From the perspective of the highest dimension of Buddhist practice, the Highest Yoga Tantra, there is no distinction between gender. Even in that final life in which you attain Buddhahood, there is no difference whether you are male or female.

There are more female concerns in this system. For example, one of the root downfalls is for a male to abuse or to look down upon a female. If a man does that, it is disastrous. There is no comparable downfall for a woman looking down on a man. So we men are jealous.

It is not enough to be compassionate. You must act. There are two aspects to action. One is to overcome the distortions and afflictions of your own mind, that is, in terms of calming and eventually dispelling anger. This is action out of compassion. The other is more social, more public. When something needs to be done in the world to rectify the wrongs, if one is really concerned with benefitting others, one needs to be engaged, involved.

I normally recommend to Buddhist practitioners not to see every action of their spiritual teacher as divine and noble. There are specific, very demanding qualities that are required of a spiritual mentor. You don't simply say, "It is good behavior because it is the guru's." This is never done. You should recognize the unwholesome as being unwholesome, so one might infer that it is worthwhile to criticize it.

If one feels very profound compassion, this already implies an intimate connection with another person. It is said in our scriptures that we are to cultivate love just like that of a mother toward her only child. This is very intimate. The Buddhist notion of attachment is not what people in the West assume. We say that the love of a mother for her only child is free of attachment.

People should remain in society and carry out their usual profession. While contributing to society, they should internally carry on analysis and practice. In daily life, one should go to the office, work, and return home. It would be worthwhile to sacrifice some late evening entertainment, go to sleep early, and get up early the next morning to perform analytical meditation.

To help others in the most effective way possible we have to be fully enlightened buddhas. Even to help others in vast and extensive ways we need to have attained one of the levels of a bodhisattva, that is, to have had the experience of a direct, nonconceptual reality of voidness and to have achieved the powers of extrasensory perception. Nonetheless, there are many levels of help we can offer others.

From one point of view we can say that we have human bodies and are practicing the Buddha's teachings and are thus much better than insects. But from another view we can say that insects are very innocent and free from guile, whereas we often lie and misrepresent ourselves in devious ways in order to achieve our ends or better ourselves. From this perspective, we are much worse than insects, who just go about their business without pretending to be anything.

In this age of degeneration when one meets with all sorts of problems and adverse circumstances, the practice of generating positive thoughts is very effective. If someone lacks this practice, even though that person might be a very serious meditator, he or she will meet with many hardships and hurdles.

Let us examine what "I" or "self" is. What is definite is that it does not exist independently of our body and mind. And out of the two, the body and mind, it is clear that the body cannot be seen as this "self." Feelings are also not the self because there is a "feeler" and a feeling. Also, the way we naturally perceive ourselves, the way the sense of "self" arises, is that there is something like the agent or the subject, which experiences and perceives. So to our naive, natural mind, everything appears as if it has an independent, solid, objective entity or objective status. However, what is very clear is that when we begin to search, they disintegrate and disappear, and they are unfindable.

We are all on this planet together. We are all brothers and sisters with the same physical and mental faculties, the same problems, and the same needs. We must all contribute to the fulfillment of the human potential and the improvement of the quality of life as much as we are able. Mankind is crying out for help. Ours is a desperate time. Those who have something to offer should come forward. Now is the time.

DECEMBER 17

If you know that someone is speaking badly of you behind your back, and if you react to that negativity with a feeling of hurt, then you destroy your own peace of mind. One's pain is one's own creation. One should treat such things as if they are wind behind one's ear. In other words, just brush them aside.

To a large extent, whether or not one suffers pain depends on how one responds to a given situation. What makes a difference is whether or not one is too sensitive and takes things too seriously.

In most cases the affirmation of the ego leads only to disappointment, or else to conflict with other egos just as exclusive as mine—especially when the strong development of the ego leads to whims and demands. The illusion of the permanent self secretes a danger that lies in wait for all of us: I want this, I want that. You might end up killing someone, as we all know well.

The excess of egoism leads to uncontrollable perversions, which always end badly. But from another standpoint, a firm ego, sure of itself, can be a very positive element. You have to have real confidence in yourself.

You have to understand that the affection I am speaking of has no purpose, it is not given with the intention of getting anything back. It is not a matter of feeling. In the same way we say that real compassion is without attachment. Pay attention to this point, which goes against our habitual ways of thinking. It is not this or that particular case that stirs our pity. We don't give our compassion to such and such a person by choice. We give it spontaneously, entirely, without hoping for anything in exchange. And we give it universally.

DECEMBER 20

If I die in exile, and if the Tibetan people wish to continue the institution of the Dalai Lama, my reincarnation will not be born under Chinese control.

With the love that is simply attachment, the slightest change in the object, such as a tiny change of attitude, immediately causes you to change. This is because your emotion is based on something very superficial. Take, for example, a new marriage.

Often after a few weeks, months, or years the couple become enemies and finish up getting divorced. They married deeply in love—nobody marries with hatred—but after a short time everything changed. Why?

Some psychologists say that we should not repress anger but express it—that we should practice anger! Here we should make a distinction between mental problems that should and should not be expressed. Sometimes you may be truly wronged and it is right for you to express your grievance instead of letting it fester inside you. But you should not express it with anger.

If you go more deeply into your own spiritual practice, emphasizing wisdom and compassion, you will encounter the suffering of other sentient beings again and again, and you will have the capacity to acknowledge it, respond to it, and feel deep compassion rather than apathy or impotence.

When contemplating suffering, do not fall into the feeling of self-importance or conceit. Cultivating wisdom helps us to avoid these pitfalls. But it is hard to generalize because each person's courage and forbearance are unique.

The self-cherishing attitude makes us very uptight; we think we are extremely important, and our basic desire is for ourselves to be happy and for things to go well for us. Yet we don't know how to bring this about. In fact, acting out of self-cherishing can never make us happy.

DECEMBER 25

No matter who we are with, we often think things like "I am stronger than he," "I am more beautiful than she," "I am more intelligent," "I am wealthier," "I am much better qualified," and so forth—we generate much pride. This is not good. Instead, we should always remain humble.

Even when we are helping others and are engaged in charity work, we should not regard ourselves in a very haughty way as great protectors benefitting the weak.

If you must be selfish, then be wise and not narrow-minded in your selfishness.

Whoever excludes others will find himself ex-
cluded in turn. Those who affirm that their God is
the only God are doing something dangerous and
pernicious, because they are on the way to imposing
their beliefs on others, by any means possible.

There were once two monks—a teacher and his student. In order to give some encouragement to his student, the teacher said, "One day we will definitely go for a picnic." After a few days it was forgotten. The student later reminded the teacher of his promise but the teacher responded by saying that he was too busy to go for a picnic for a while.

A long time passed; no picnic. When reminded again, the teacher said, "Not now. I am far too busy." So one day the student saw a dead body being carried off, and the teacher asked him, "What is happening?" And the student replied, "Well, that poor man is going on a picnic!" So, unless you make specific time for something that you feel committed to, you will always have other obligations.

DECEMBER 29

The essence of all spiritual life is your emotion, your attitude toward others. Once you have pure and sincere motivation, all the rest follows. You can develop this right attitude toward others on the basis of kindness, love, and respect, and on the clear realization of the oneness of all human beings.

I would like, on behalf of the Tibetans in and outside Tibet, to sincerely thank our supporters and friends. We are going through immeasurable hardship and suffering that is unprecedented in our history. The sympathy, support, and help that the people of the world, led by India, have accorded to us will forever be remembered and recorded in history.

For as long as space endures, and for as long as living beings remain, until then may I, too, abide, to dispel the misery of the world.

Index

New from Penguin

Live in a Better Way: Reflections on Truth, Love, and Happiness
His Holiness the Dalai Lama
Compiled and Edited by Renuka Singh
With an Introduction by Lama Thubten Zopa Rinpoche

Imbued with a friendly tone and pithy wisdom, this handsome handbook to approaching life "in a better way" includes six of His Holiness the Dalai Lama's inspirational public lectures. Following each talk are original question-and-answer sessions with the Dalai Lama himself as he explains, with compassionate guidance, his spiritual teachings. The book also contains a practical and accessible introduction to Buddhism and the Dalai Lama's spiritual origins written by the renowned Lama Thubten Zopa Rinpoche.

ISBN 0-14-219607-X

FOR MORE BOOKS BY AND ABOUT THE NOBEL PEACE PRIZE-WINNER, HIS HOLINESS THE DALAI LAMA, LOOK FOR THE

PENGUIN
COMPASS

Dalai Lama, My Son: A Mother's Story
Diki Tsering

In this fascinating memoir, the Dalai Lama's mother tells a compelling tale of one woman's remarkable journey. With vivid and intimate details, she recounts her life's humble beginnings, the customs and rituals of old Tibet, the births of her sixteen children (seven of which survived), learning her son's remarkable destiny, and her family's exile from Tibet with the Chinese invasion. Rich in Tibetan history and culture, this moving memoir illuminates the role of Tibetan women as well as Tibet's ancient ideals of compassion and faith through the unique perspective of the mother of an internationally beloved spiritual leader.

ISBN 0-14-019626-9